Pollen's **women**

THE ART OF SAMSON POLLEN

EDITED BY ROBERT DEIS & WYATT DOYLE

THE MEN'S ADVENTURE LIBRARY

MensPulpMags.com

#new texture

Also available from The Men's Adventure Library:
Pollen's Action
Pollen in Print 1955–1959

A New Texture book

With thanks to Jacqueline Pollen and gratitude to Rich Oberg

Archival materials provided by The Robert Deis Archive
Some pieces courtesy The David O'Dell Collection
Special research by TJ Duke

Designed by Wyatt Doyle for The Men's Adventure Library

[Instagram] @ThisIsNewTexture   NewTexture.com

MensAdventureLibrary.com   MensPulpMags.com

Booksellers: *Pollen's Women* and other New Texture books are available through Ingram Book Co.

ISBN 978-1-943444-21-2

Second printing

Printed in the United States of America

10 9 8 7 6 5 4 3 2

introduction

Artist Samson Pollen is one of the grandmasters of illustration art used for the vintage men's adventure magazines (MAMs) that flourished from the early 1950s to the mid-1970s. He also did top-notch illustration art for other types of periodicals and for paperback books. But most of Pollen's artwork—literally hundreds of paintings—was created for the Atlas/Diamond group of MAMs published by Martin Goodman's Magazine Management Company. Those included many of the best, most popular and longest running magazines in the men's adventure genre, such as *Action For Men*, *For Men Only*, *Male*, *Man's World*, *Men*, *Stag*, and *True Action*.

Pollen is currently less well known than some of the other great artists who worked for those magazines. This is largely because most examples of vintage MAM artwork shown in books and internet posts are covers, and Pollen specialized in doing interior illustrations. He did do many cover paintings for action, adventure, and romance paperbacks during his long career as an illustrator, but for MAMs, Pollen preferred—and became a go-to artist for—illustrations printed inside across the first two pages of stories.

Until now, most of the original paintings Pollen did for those two-page spreads (which were sometimes printed vertically) have never been seen. Some have been lost. Fortunately, Pollen held onto many of his originals, and others are owned by two major illustration art collectors who share our interest in increasing awareness of the men's adventure realm: David O'Dell and Rich Oberg. It was Rich who put us touch with Pollen in 2016, around the time Sam turned 86 years old.

When we asked Sam if he'd like to collaborate on collections featuring his original artwork for our Men's Adventure Library series, I was thrilled that he gave us the thumbs-up and full access to his paintings. Since then, we've had the pleasure of talking and corresponding with Sam many times.

It seemed obvious to us that one of the Pollen art books we publish should focus on his MAM artwork that features women. Images of beautiful women were common in MAMs, and Pollen was particularly adept at painting scenes that *feature* beautiful women—and he did scores of them for Goodman's Atlas/Diamond magazines.

Even the early portfolio sample painting of a group of teenage delinquents that became his first illustration in a Goodman MAM (see pg. 6) shows he had a special flair for painting female characters more complex than standard damsels in distress; Pollen's women are often powerful or dangerous or both. Some are temptresses or femme fatales, seeking to lure a man into doing their bidding. Others are warriors, fighting alongside (or against) the male characters in the scene. There are also women in some Pollen illustrations who are relegated to being helpmates to the male protagonists. Some are simply unashamedly sexually aggressive.

But, while MAMs are of their time and thus not particularly evolved in terms of perspectives on gender roles or sexuality (despite occasional unexpectedly advanced thinking in those areas), Pollen's women are almost never helpless victims. They also contradict the widespread misperception that MAM illustrations typically show women being abused. In fact, "bondage and torture"-style stories and artwork were only prevalent in the "sweat mag" subgenre of MAMs, which account for less than a third of the more than 160 different MAM titles that were published—and even less of the total readership. The Atlas/Diamond group Samson Pollen worked for (and most other mid- and top-tier MAMs) didn't feature such stuff.

Another revelation comes from being able to see Pollen's original MAM paintings. They are far more lush and painterly than you can tell from seeing them in magazine spreads, surrounded by headlines, subheads and text, and printed on medium- to low-quality paper. Samson Pollen's paintings stand on their own as artwork. As illustration art, they also tell stories.

Artists in the realm of "fine arts" can generally choose the scenes they paint, and their paintings may or may not try to convey a story about what's portrayed. Professional illustrators are hired to depict scenes to accompany specific stories. Yet within the boundaries of those limitations, top illustrators like Samson Pollen are able to use their skill and imagination to create exceptional art.

Artists who created men's adventure mag illustrations were given little to go on as far as the stories they were illuminating (usually no more than a one to three sentence description of the story), and minimal guidance from the magazine's art director on what setting, action and characters he wanted depicted. The artist was then expected to do initial sketches, take any reference photos of models he needed, and submit a finished painting in a matter of days.

Instead of being hamstrung by the strictures of illustrating stories, Pollen soared. It was a challenge on many levels, but one that Sam not only rose to again and again, but relished. Per Sam:

"They might say something like 'Well, the hero has an automatic weapon in one hand and he's carrying a woman in another hand and she's holding a dog and they're climbing up a cliff.' So I'd have to come up with a solution. What I would do is visualize it. I'd try to look at the scene as I'd see it in my imagination. That's the part I liked the most: Trying to make sense out of something and create a story of it in my mind, then translate that into a painting."

We love the paintings Samson Pollen created as a result of that process, and we believe he deserves wider recognition as an artist. Our hope is that this book will help make that happen.

—*Bob Deis*
Somewhere near Key West, Dec. 2017

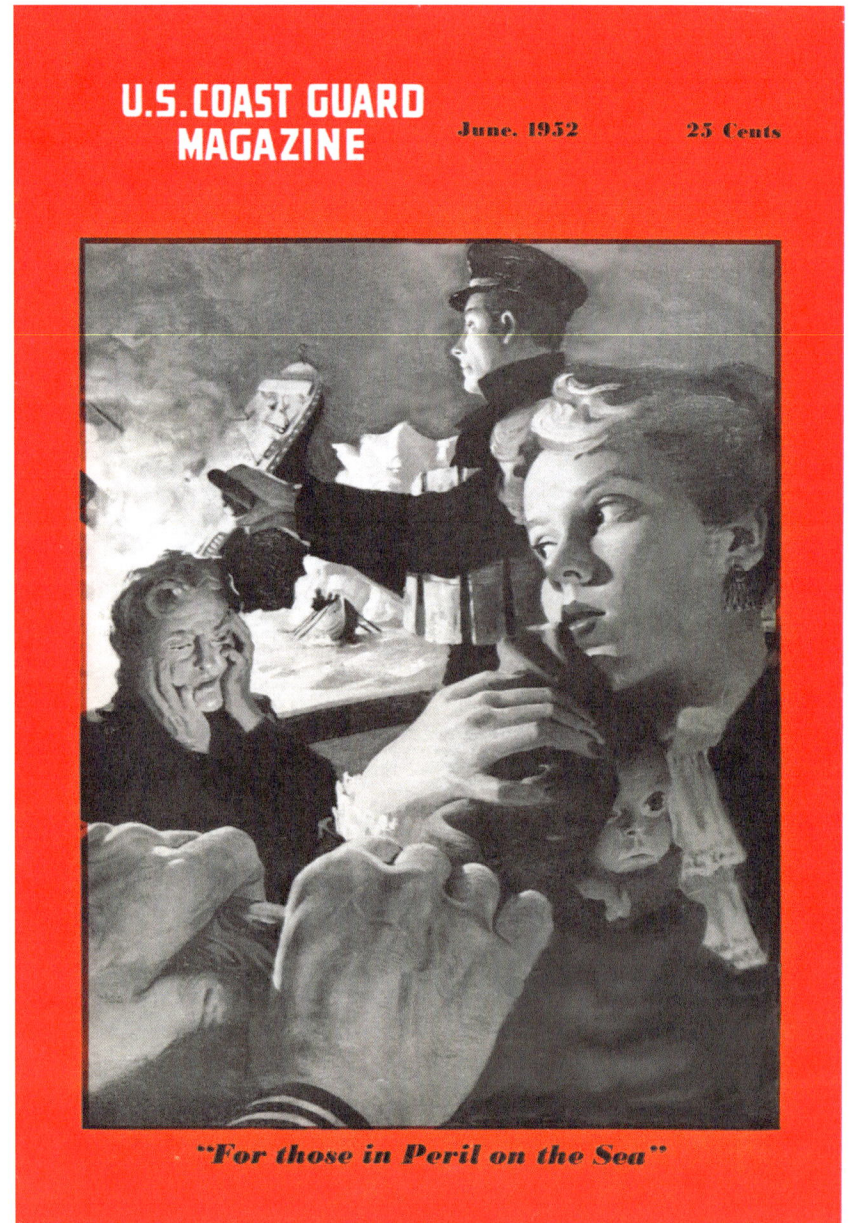

U.S. Coast Guard Magazine, June 1952
"For Those in Peril on the Sea"

Painted women

MY FIRST crush was a girl named Matilda. She wore a sailor outfit, like kids wore in those days: dark pleated skirt, sailor collar and stripes. I ran up, pulled her pigtails and ran away—but I never even spoke to her, not once. That's the way kids are who are shy, when they have their first run-in with women, with girls.

I grew up in a good atmosphere, with my mother and sister. I think my mother was a natural born psychiatrist; she knew how to handle people. I never remember her yelling, or raising her voice at anybody. Yet she was strong, and got what she wanted without yelling or threatening—just using common sense. She had a natural ability that way. My sister, too; she became a teacher.

I WAS in the Coast Guard Reserve. I knew I'd be drafted, and I didn't want to live in a foxhole. A ship is a lot cleaner; you've got a mattress and a sheet. When I was drafted, I went to the headquarters on Canal Street with a few pieces of my work, which I showed to one of the officers. He brought in a higher ranking officer and I ended up going up the chain to the admiral's office. The admiral said, "Well, before you do any artwork or anything, I want you to get some salt in your blood." He wanted me to be on a ship, to be a Coast Guardsman first. So I served overseas: Staten Island. (To me, I was overseas once I was over the Hudson River.)

I wanted more of a challenge. Working for the government, you could be kind of lax; smoke a pipe, work a little, and take the rest of the day off…. I thought it was a dead end, as far as art goes. Towards the end, they gave me a studio. It was huge. It was the size of a gym, an enormous auditorium. I had this huge studio, and I had the freedom to go for art supplies. I'd drive out in the jeep—they gave me a jeep!—and go to the art store. I'd leave the base at two in the afternoon, come and go as I pleased, and nobody complained. I'm an artist, right? I've got moods. People think of artists as moody people, you

know? You've got to let them do their thing. I took advantage of that!

I did the *Titanic* for the cover of *Coast Guard Magazine*. They really liked it. In the painting, I focused on a rowboat, up close: a woman holding a baby, an elderly woman crying, and the yeoman up there, steering the oars. I put a human touch to it. I wanted to tell a story, so I played up the human interest and that's why they liked it, I guess. I was becoming an illustrator then.

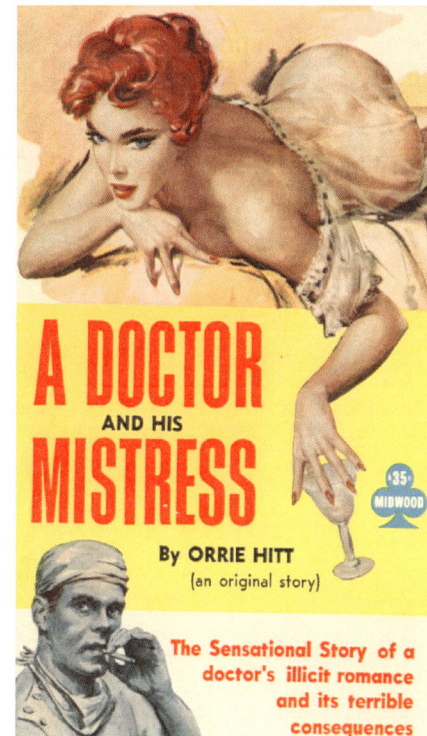

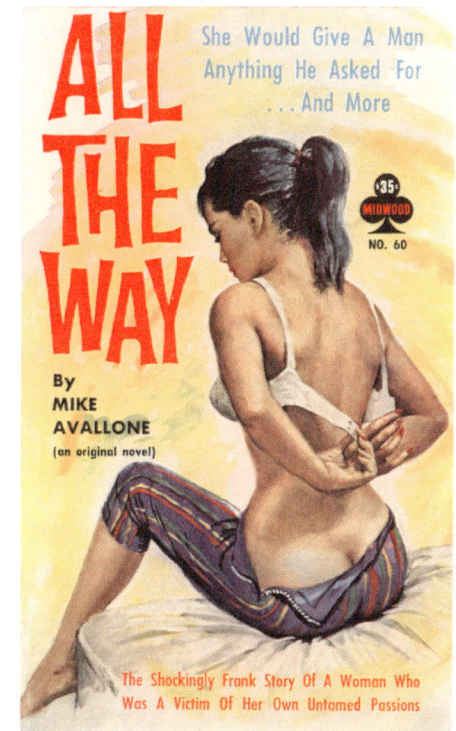

Paperback covers by Pollen for Midwood: Orrie Hitt's *A Doctor and His Mistress* (1960) and *All the Way* (1962) by Mike Avallone

"I'd just come out of the service, and I needed a sample to show. I made this painting on my own time, and the reason it's one of my better ones is because that was one I handled like Norman Rockwell would handle his work: You do a careful sketch, you do a thorough drawing…you do all those things that prepare you to do a better painting. I didn't have any editors or an author telling me what to do; it was strictly mine. I took as long as I wanted. I even got real characters, which I don't bother with usually; I'd just hire a standard commercial model. But I went to a poolroom to get real teenagers that really looked the part. And they *acted* the part—they were tough guys.

"It was meant as a sample, but [Magazine Management art director] Mel Blum liked it and used it for a story. So my first sample was bought and I worked from there on, you know? I didn't have to shop around. I was pretty fortunate that way.

"They blew it up and put it across two pages. But it wasn't meant to be split up; it was not a spread. They split it in a bad place and they cut the bottom half of the painting out. You're missing the legs, which I think are important to the painting. That was a disappointment.

"I got credited for it in print: ART BY SAMSON POLLEN, in little letters underneath the illustration.

"One of the poolroom guys had a lawyer in the family, and he sued [MM publisher] Martin Goodman for using his image without a model release. You had to have signed permission to use their picture commercially. But I didn't know about that.

"Martin Goodman was really good to me on that, maybe because he liked my work. He said that he'd take a certain amount out of each job he gave me, and I'd pay it off that way. But he never took a penny. They made some arrangement, I guess, and I never had to pay anything. He had his own lawyers, you know.

"That's a hell of a way to get started, right?"

WHEN I was in my late teens and started to paint, I couldn't afford models; I didn't go that route. I just got a couple of kids from the neighborhood and took their pictures—reference photos. I started a couple of them on their careers, actually. Later on in life they were very successful at what they did—theater, movies, Hollywood.

There are certain characteristics that these gals had that made them decide to model. They liked a lot of attention. They were always the life of the party, and it was hello to everyone as they walked down the street…they'd be waving to everybody.

Iris Menshell was like that, I used her a few times. She lived across the street. She was friendly and lively, she really had what it took. Later, she used a different name and took on a French accent. When she came back to the neighborhood, she put her hand out elegantly and asked me to kiss her hand—with a French accent, like she's French! She was unbelievable. But she was a beautiful girl. Years later, I saw her in a couple of Western films. [Menshell worked in film and television as Lita Milan. —Ed.]

Louisa Moritz (One Flew Over the Cuckoo's Nest, Death Race 2000) was another model. She was on TV a lot at the time. Her specialty was children's voices; she was really believable. She wanted to move in with me. Nothing to do with love, or anything like that; she wanted a place where she could keep costumes and stuff. It was the convenience of my apartment that interested her! She was really a live wire, very friendly. I thought she was nice.

Cathy Joyce lived around the corner. She'd wear a ball cap pulled down over her eyes, glasses…you wouldn't believe she was a model. But when she made herself up and got in front of a camera, she was beautiful. She made most of her money on the weekend, as a belly dancer. She danced in a nightclub. She invited me one time, and boy was she good! The costumes, the color, the movement….

Ellen Burstyn, the actress, was the secretary for Scott Photography on Madison Avenue—Edna. [Burstyn was born Edna Rae Gillooly. —Ed.] She was pretty, and she filled in if a model didn't show up and they needed someone quickly.

Shere Hite was one of my models, she lived close by. She went on to write The Hite Report, Oedipus Revisited…. She was quite some character, believe me. One time I had her in my studio with [iconic illustration model] Steve Holland, and Steve was a macho guy—a real nice guy, but kind of macho. And she was Women's Lib all the way, so there was a little clash. And they're

Portrait of the artist as a young man: Samson Pollen at 18.

7

arguing and arguing…. They had a fight, and she walked out, in the middle of a modeling session. Pretty unusual! She wrote me a postcard. She said she lost her temper, she didn't mean it and so forth.

I never really wanted to mix with models. As long as they were nice, I liked them. But a lot of them had big egos. Maybe that's why they go into that field—they like the spotlight. That type really didn't interest me, very ambitious people. I could never warm up to them. I like more down-to-earth people.

Some men, like my ex-father-in-law, kept asking me, "When are you gonna let me hold the lights when you shoot a job?" They all wanted to meet these models, you know, from Wilhelmina and Ford and whatnot. But I didn't have the wide assortment of models that they thought I had. I'd change their looks, their faces…I could get a variety of characters from a single model.

Sometimes you'd get somebody who'd cry to you, or complain the lights are too hot, or they wouldn't come on time…. I'd stick with the ones who had proven themselves with other illustrators. They had to be dependable, that's very important. And when I was shooting, I didn't want any disturbances.

They're very expensive, models. If you start gabbing or having coffee or getting too friendly, you're not getting the job done. The hour or two is gone, and then you rush to get pictures, which don't come out so good because you didn't focus on it. Start getting too personal, you're ruining the job. You're shooting for the wrong purpose.

So I spent most of the allotted time getting through whatever work I had set aside for the model. And I'd make sure there was no interference and nobody in the room to disturb us. Sure, I could have shot more nudes if I'd wanted to. But I knew that would be a big distraction for everybody, and then when I'd get the photos back, I wouldn't have what I wanted for the job. Mostly I had them wear bikinis, because there's freedom for movement but no self-consciousness. I tried to keep it businesslike. You're doing a job and you've got a deadline, and you've got to get it done right. I didn't want to be diverted from that.

I DON'T remember the magazines' art directors ever telling us what the women should look like. They were more interested in the details, the subject

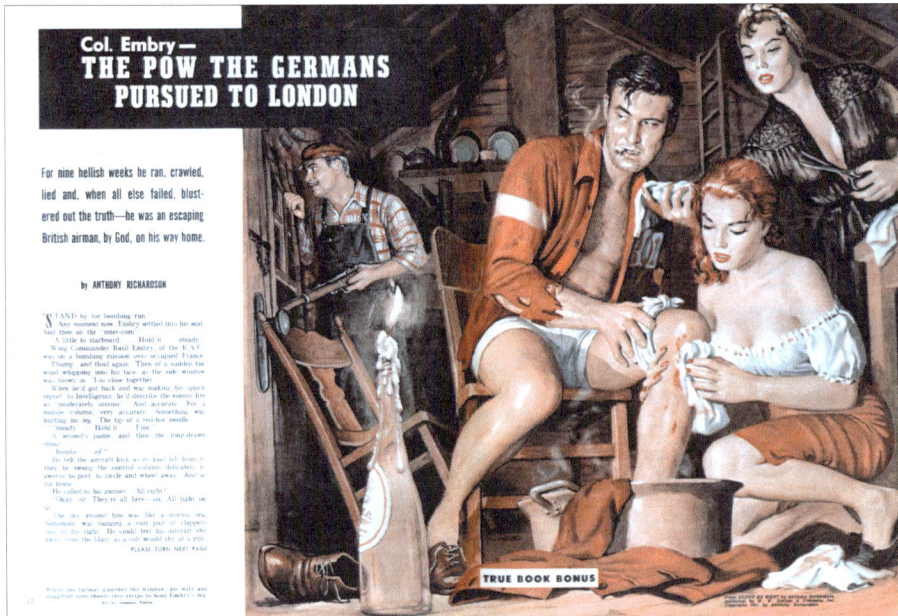

Ken For Men, May 1959
"The POW The Germans Pursued to London"

Male, November 1956
"The Strange Women"

"This painting was done under unusual circumstances. When the adventure magazines faded away, I left illustration painting to run a color separation business; I wanted to get out of the house. I kept it running for a few years, then one of my friends called me and said boy, you've got to come back to paperbacks, it's booming! Being as I'd been away a bit, I needed something to show. They were doing Gothic illustrations at the time—the ones with the bedroom light upstairs in the castle, and the cloudiness and all that. So I made this quickly, and from there on it was smooth sailing. At CBS they had a book division, and I got right into that—but no Gothics! So out of something like 500 paintings I've done, it's the only one—I think—that was not reproduced. Because it was not done as an assignment, it was done as a sample.

"That is the one painting I did of Jackie [Jacqueline Pollen, Sam's wife]. She didn't model for me much. She was out working, doing her thing. She had a job she liked. Why should she bang her head against the wall, carrying around a composite book to show modeling samples, all that? It's a different world. Besides, the publishers were paying [for professional models and reference photography], so let them do the work, and let them pay for it! She was always very pretty, she just didn't go that route.

"I'm married to Jackie 40 years; she's an angel. We met at an event—a social, where you meet people. Jackie's mother had insisted she go. My sister had insisted I go. She did her mother a favor and I did my sister a favor. Jackie walked into the room like a ballerina. She had long, long hair and these big eyes…. I was the first one to go over and talk to her, and here we are, 40 years later. I was lucky, I found the right person. I hit the jackpot—the Jackie-pot!

"We still feel when we go out to dinner or something that it's like a date. We are who we are, and we don't go out of our way to 'be' anything, or to pretend. By the time you get married, you're already well established in terms of your personality, your character and so forth. You bring to marriage what you are. I like to have fun, I kid around a lot…I'm not a sourpuss, that's for sure. Some people make too big a deal out of everything. Fall into it, let it ride by itself. Leave it go, let it go smoothly, let it flow. And that's what we've done.

"You meet someone, you don't know what's going to happen. I threw the dice, and it came out good."

matter, the story, the composition…there were a whole lot of things they were looking at besides the women. They *expect* the women to be pretty. If you do an ugly woman, you're not going to get any assignments! So it's assumed that you're doing a decent job on the women—and that's important. The women sell the product; we know that. Look at every ad on television. People like sexy women! That's good, it makes the world go 'round.

Supposedly, I did sexy women. They never complained about my women. Actually, I kept getting work for that reason. And I was reliable, too. That's a thing some artists are underrated on, their reliability. An art director wants to know if he's got a deadline and he gives an artist the assignment, he'll be able to walk in to the editor and the publisher with a painting he can be proud of. It's a reflection on them. He's always thinking in terms of where he stands, and I understand that. So I was never bothered by editorial criticism. I felt, coming from professionals, it was helpful. I knew they were going for

a certain objective, and often they made sense. If you're gonna get a big ego and feel that criticism is a personal attack, you're in the wrong field, that's for sure. That's why I lasted so long.

Because nothing was regular at the time, I never knew what day of the week it was. I didn't know if it was Wednesday or Saturday, because all days were the same. I had different deadlines. Sometimes I had to work on the weekend, and other times I had a couple of days off. So there was enough variety to keep it interesting. And I liked that. At heart, I'm not a 9-to-5 man.

The time it took to complete a painting varied tremendously. There's one piece I remember that set a record in my book. They were in a terrible rush, so I went into the art director's office at Magazine Management and did a pencil sketch of the idea, right there on the spot; it took me 15 minutes. I went home, got the model, shot reference photos and did the developing and everything—it takes a long time! Then I did the painting and delivered it the

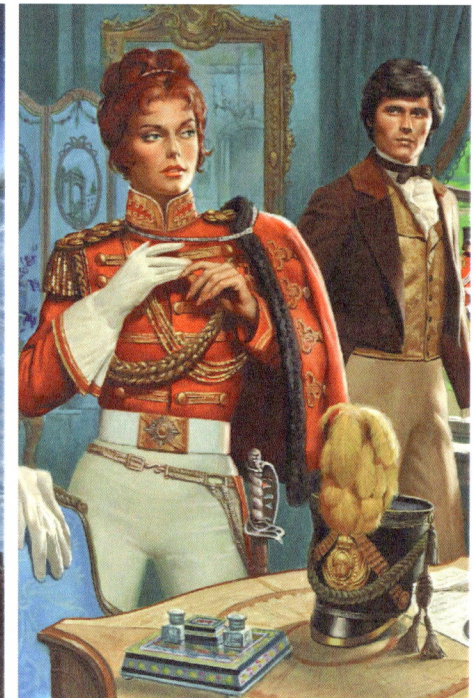

"I'd do a kids' book, then an action series, romance novels…I was moving from one to another quite comfortably. I didn't think much about it; it was still the same technique. I think it was instinctive. For romance, you want romance! So it wasn't wild action, it was holding hands, embraces, looking at each other romantically, that type of thing. And costumes—they like to see the detail in the dresses and so forth. But it wasn't a big move for me to go from one to the other. I just kept painting the way I always painted."

next morning. I was up all night painting.

Sometimes they wanted changes. If it was a big enough change, you'd go home and work on it. If it was a small change, you'd go to the art department. They had the brushes, they had the paints, and you could touch it up there, without that extra trip home and back. But I kind of enjoyed the trips. At the time I had a sports car, and I loved to drive it. I'd put the painting in the back, with the top down… it wasn't a bad drive. I was so busy, it was one of the few chances I'd get to drive that car; when I sold it, it only had 5,000 miles on it. There's a lot of work in being an illustrator if you want to do it well.

It was a good life. I worked long hours; I probably worked harder than other people—most illustrators do. I'm not one of those artists that goes around pouting all the time that they had a rough life, that they're doing all this art because they're suffering so much. So maybe I'm not a true artist, because I don't fit the bill there. There's this idea of artists sitting in Greenwich Village with berets and handlebar mustaches, just talking politics all the time. But that doesn't apply to illustrators at all. They work hard; it's a job. You can't just sit down and talk about your painting and go on for hours discussing what the meaning is. You can't! You've got to sit down and *produce* and deliver the job on time.

You're looking at the paintings differently than I do. When you produce them, you see all the petty little things. Someone who only sees the final product sees something completely different. They don't see the toil, the sketches, the errors, the changes, the deadlines, the frustrations, and all the other things that might go into a painting. It's made up of a lot of things, that painting.

—*Samson Pollen, as told to Wyatt Doyle*

"I did a movie poster of Ursula Andress in the jungle (*Slave of the Cannibal God*, 1978). I wasn't into movie posters, but in this case, I did one. All they gave me for reference was a little wallet-sized headshot. That's all I had, and I had a to put a body on her. Stacy Keach was in the background. I don't even know where it is now! So a lot of my work, particularly in the early days, I never got back. I have only the proofs, the covers, but I don't have the original artwork."

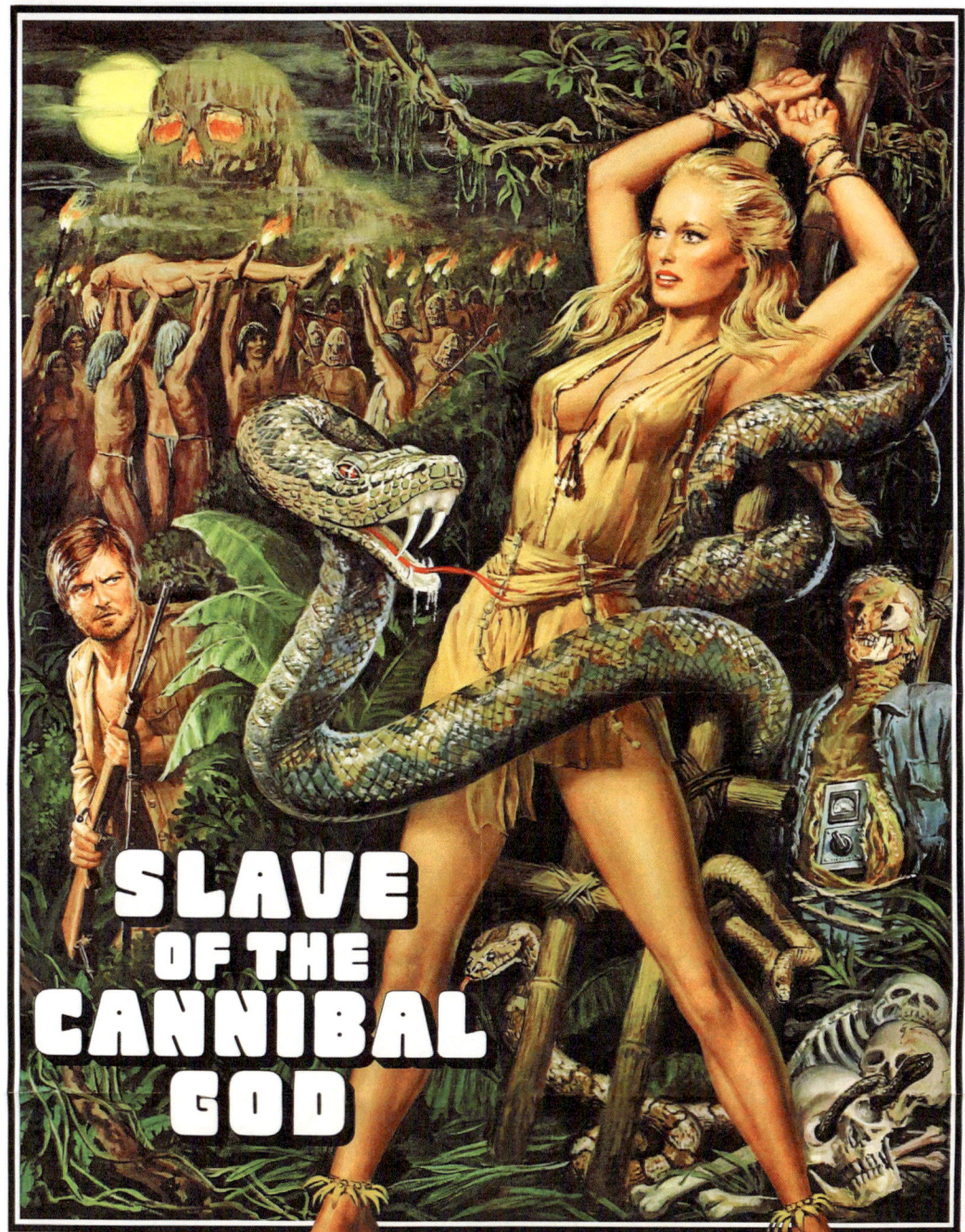

"SLAVE OF
THE CANNIBAL GOD"

STARRING STACY KEACH · URSULA ANDRESS
CLAUDIO CASSINELLI

FILMED IN THE SAVAGE
AND UNEXPLORED JUNGLES
OF NEW GUINEA!

Produced by DANIA FILM-MEDUSA DISTRIBUTION · Directed by SERGIO MARTINO · EASTMANCOLOR
From NEW LINE CINEMA

R RESTRICTED
UNDER 17 REQUIRES ACCOMPANYING
PARENT OR ADULT GUARDIAN

COPYRIGHT © MCMLXXIX NEW LINE CINEMA/ALL RIGHTS RESERVED

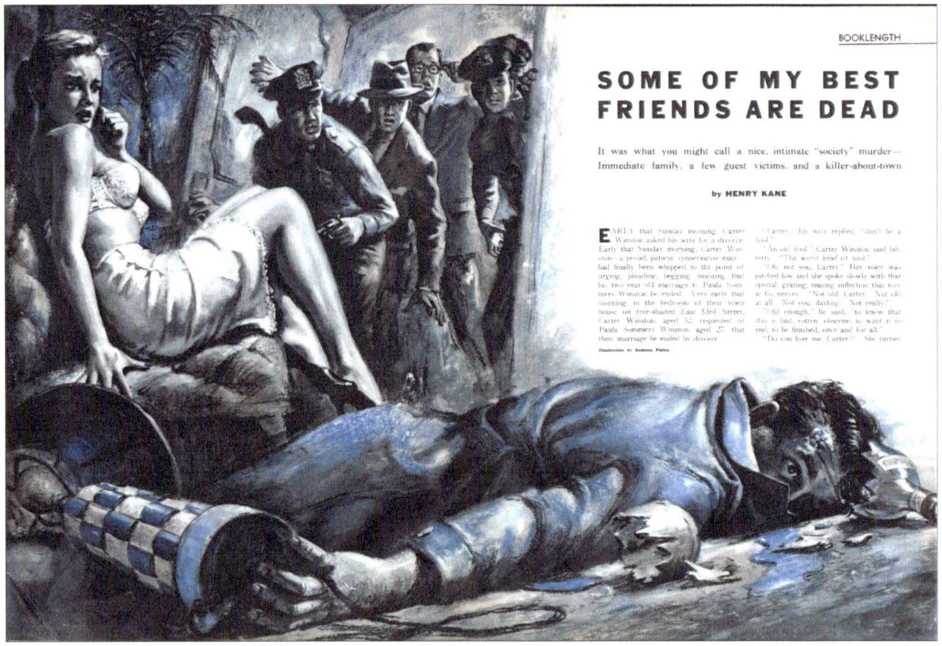

Swank
March 1958
"Some of My Best Friends Are Dead"

Man's World
December 1958
"The Fraulein Spy Who Seduced Hitler"

Men
September 1962
"The Passionate Pushover"

Male
May 1962
"The Reluctant Nymph"

Roaring Joe Boyle:
WOMAN-HUNTER, WARRIOR,
CZAR OF THE PACIFIC

Male
June 1960
"Roaring Joe Boyle: Woman-Hunter,
Warrior, Czar of the Pacific"

THE HELL-RAISING NURSES IN
RUSSIA'S FOUL-UP COMBAT FLEET

by MIKE DOYLE

Stag
October 1960
"The Hell-Raising Nurses in
Russia's Foul-Up Combat Fleet"

Men

May 1959

"The Plot to Bury China in Money"

Male

March 1958

*"The Terrible Turk and
His Underwater Harem"*

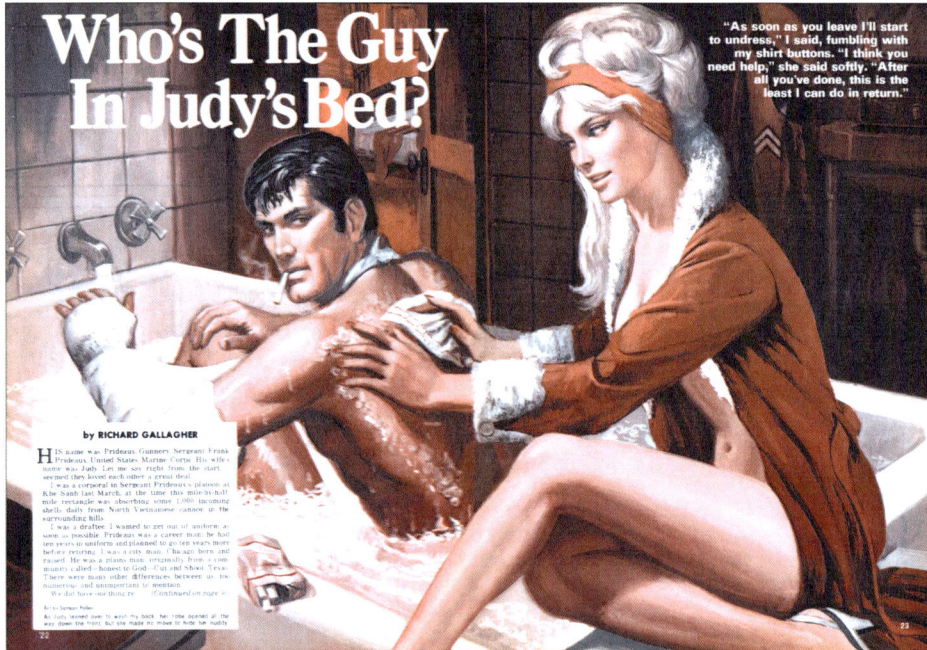

Who's The Guy In Judy's Bed?

"As soon as you leave I'll start to undress," I said, fumbling with my shirt buttons. "I think you need help," she said softly. "After all you've done, this is the least I can do in return."

by RICHARD GALLAGHER

HIS name was Prideaux. Gunnery Sergeant Frank Prideaux United States Marine Corps. His wife's name was Judy. Let me say right from the start, seemed they loved each other a great deal.

I was a corporal in Sergeant Prideaux's platoon at Khe Sanh last March, at the time this mile-by-half mile rectangle was absorbing some 1,000 incoming shells daily from North Vietnamese cannon in the surrounding hills.

I was a drafter. I wanted to get out of uniform as soon as possible Prideaux was a career man; he had ten years in uniform and planned to go ten years more before retiring. I was a city man, Chicago born and raised. He was a plains man, originally from a community called—honest to God—Cut and Shoot Texas. There were many other differences between us too numerous and unimportant to mention.

We did have one thing in common (Continued on page...)

Moving the roller, Eddie half turned to see Vera standing in the doorway. The flush of her nakedness hit him with a jolt.

Art by Samson Pollen

by NOEL KRAFT

SUMMER COTTAGE TEASE

For three years Vera Collins had been an ache in Eddie Kojac's gut. "I'll give you what you want," she had said to him many times, "if you'll beg for it." But Eddie wouldn't beg, couldn't, and on the last day of the season, found he didn't have to . . .

SHIFTING the tool box from his right hand to the left, the husky young man rapped twice on the partially opened cottage door. Overhead, blistering summer sunshine flooded the parched Pennsylvania countryside in a blaze of golden light. Wiping the perspiration from his forehead, he waited a few moments before knocking again. This time he heard a slight movement from within. He guessed it came from the bedroom that faced the small lake, her room, and he stiffened slightly as he heard the sound of approaching footsteps.

"That you Eddie?" she called out.

He grunted in reply, and then the door opened wide and she was looking up at him.

"It's the damn shower head again," she said impatiently. "That's the second time this month."

Angry as she was, it didn't spoil her exceptionally good looks. About 22, a silky haired, blue-eyed blonde, her brief, terry cloth sarong clung (Continued on page...)

Stag

September 1968

"Who's the Guy in Judy's Bed?"

Stag

April 1967

"Summer Cottage Tease"

Stag

December 1972

"Johnny Calhoun's Girls"

Stag

December 1965

"Last Wild Fling of Daisy Bedford"

The Moonshiner's Daughter...
The Ex-Fiancee...
The Red-Headed Do-Gooder...
The "Residents" At
Maybelle Harper's Place...

JOHNNY CALHOUN'S GIRLS

PRE-MOVIE BOOK BONUS

By LARRY POWELL

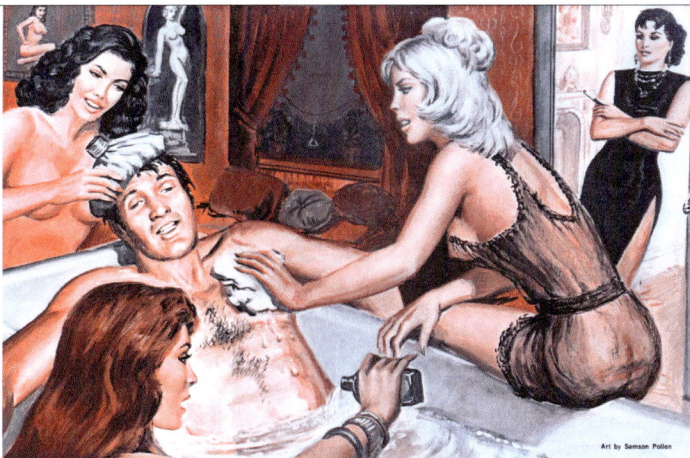

Art by Samson Pollen

Maybelle Harper's girls had themselves a ball with Johnny. They fussed and fondled him like they were his own private harem.

From the first day Johnny showed up back in town, the juices started running in every female on both sides of the tracks.

"DO YOU THINK Johnny Boy will come home?" asked Annie Ruth. Annie Ruth was 19 years old and growing in every direction, especially in the front.

"More than likely," said Nathan, her father, regarding her with suspicion. "Don't you be hanging around him when he does. Why don't you button up that blouse?"

"I can't button it. I'm too big in front."

"Then get another blouse."

Nathan had just run off another load of first class moonshine, probably the best in south Georgia, and now he was home to relax.

Annie Ruth got up and walked to her room. She closed the door, undressed in the dark and stretched out on the bed. It was hot and she was wearing only a pair of panties. A night breeze crept in the window and touched her body. She widened her thighs and sighed. She got prickly all over when she *(Continued on page 93)*

Nathan took one look at Annie Ruth sitting half-undressed on Johnny's lap and bellowed, "Johnny Boy, you son-of-a-bitch!"

The Cadillac rammed into the pile of cars, flipping Edward Tate out. He grabbed a jack handle and came after Johnny

20

21

She walked out on her job as an airlines hostess and into my hotel room the same night. Standing close to me, slightly drunk, I could barely hear her as she whispered softly, "Now, get me out of this uniform so I can't disgrace it any further."

LAST WILD FLING OF DAISY BEDFORD

by RICHARD GALLAGHER

ALL flights out of New York were grounded. Snow. Thirteen inches of snow that December 24, and still falling with the promise of perhaps another thirteen inches to come.

Even with computers, radar and snow removal equipment all of United Airlines and all of LaGuardia Airport could not promise me Joe Corone a plane to Chicago in time to see my father for Christmas.

Instead they offered everyone on Flight 131, rooms at local hotels at airline expense till the snow quit. For me they had a deluxe single at a hotel a few miles from the airport.

I picked up my reservation chit at the United desk, then walked through the slashing snow to the Terminal bar to have a drink under the plastic trees and watch the snow removal crews do foolish battle with the drifts swirling around the runways. I was in no hurry to spend the rest of Christmas Eve by myself in a hotel room. At the moment I was lonely, a classic case of Alone-on-Christmas Blues. I wanted desperately to be home for this holiday and now it seemed as though I wouldn't be.

It had been four years to this very Christmas since I had seen my father. Four *(Continued on page 56)*

Art by Samson Pollen

I sat on the edge of the tub and watched her bathe. She smiled and said, "Scrub your back for a nickel, mister."

32

29

Stag
November 1966
"The Fraulein Trap"

True Action
October 1973
"Peggy's Wildest Summer"

For Men Only
December 1964
"Afternoon With an Off-Limit Redhead"

SEX FICTION

By ALEX AUSTIN

"SURE I'M a bitch," she said, smiling at Lou. "But a good man likes to tame a bitch like me, doesn't he?"

Lou continued working on the washing machine valve he had been called in to repair.

Mrs. Kate Foster was standing beside him, wearing a white bikini that looked as if it had been made of two or three handkerchiefs. Her gorgeous body was well-tanned. Her blonde hair hung half-way down her back.

"Or are you a moral man?" she asked Lou.

He put the wrench back in his tool box, stood up. *(Continued on page 50)*

Lou was there only to fix the shower head, but Mrs. Alberts had better uses for his talents.

Knowing how to handle wrench and hammer is one thing, but coping with vacationing wenches is another matter altogether . . .

THE SPOILED SUMMER TRAMP

For Men Only

September 1973

"The Spoiled Summer Tramp"

He'd been wheeling his rig for three days, and Bunny promised to help him unwind. "There's a lot you need to know about men," he warned the eager blonde. "And boy, am I in the mood to learn," the girl shot back.

by BARRY JAMIESON

Joe never obeyed the rules of the road—so why start now with this girl? "Come on in," Bunny said playfully.

PASSIONATE PICKUP ON ROUTE 101

JOE GRUNSTON had passed the area many times before. First came the curve on Highway 101, then a stretch of woods, and finally the cluster of two-story brick buildings surrounded by wisteria and weeping willow. He shifted the trailer rig into lower gear, eased down on the air brakes, and flicked his eyes at the women's college.

The students moved stiffly on the campus books cuddled against their chests, chins lifted. In the chilly months, they wore dirty tan raincoats, scuffed loafers, and dark knee socks. In warm weather they had on white blouses, loose skirts, and no socks with their loafers. They rarely smiled, or showed any sign that they were enjoying themselves. Joe Grunston couldn't imagine what their lives were like off the campus. What kind of pajamas did they *(Continued on page 85)*

For Men Only

February 1965

"Passionate Pickup on Route 101"

35

From An Amazing
Jungle Trek Diary

EXPEDITION
to the
"STRANGE
WOMEN" TRIBE
OF NEW GUINEA

STORY STARTS ON NEXT PAGE▶

Stag

February 1968

"Expedition to the 'Strange Women'
Tribe of New Guinea"

Amazing Jungle Trek Discovery

SEDUCTION
VILLAGE OF
STONE AGE
SHE-DEVILS

No chance of es-
cape, they were
trapped in a land
where an unknown
disease drove
women to orgias-
tic frenzies of
slaughter and sex.

by CARL SHERMAN

For Men Only Annual No. 6

1970

"Seduction Village of Stone Age She-Devils"

TWO BACHELORS REPORT:

"We were Shipwrecked
on an All-Girl Island"

By EVAN TEEL and PRITCHARD RILEY

Bachelor

July 1958

"We Were Shipwrecked on an All-Girl Island"

Stag
October 1966
"Trek to the World's Most Savage Tribes"

For Men Only
February 1958
"Love Paradise of the Shipwrecked GI"

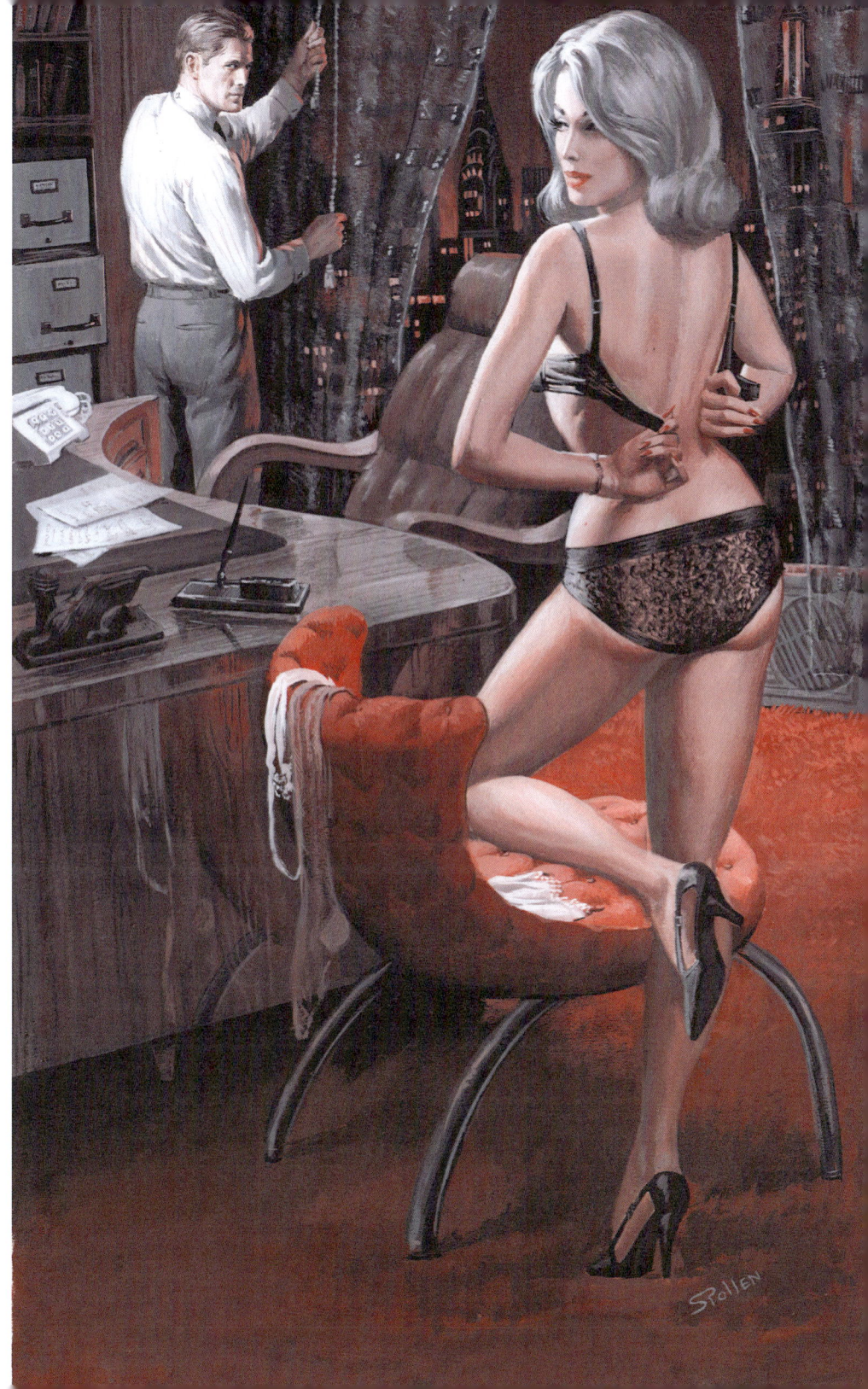

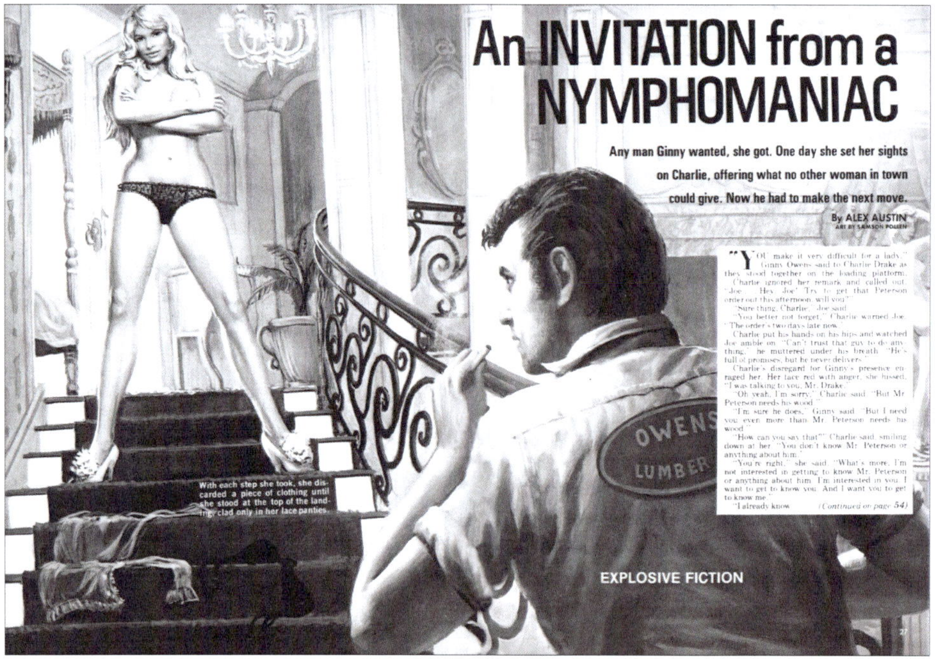

An INVITATION from a NYMPHOMANIAC

Any man Ginny wanted, she got. One day she set her sights on Charlie, offering what no other woman in town could give. Now he had to make the next move.

By ALEX AUSTIN
ART BY SAMSON POLLEN

EXPLOSIVE FICTION

Bugsy Siegel

EVER-LOVIN' TOP GUN OF THE SYNDICATE

Blasting his way up from New York's gutters to a directorship in Luciano's crime cartel, this handsome killer "organized" Hollywood—and the movie colony loved it. But when he tried to convert Las Vegas into a gambling mecca, he made one fatal mistake.

by ANTHONY SCADUTO

THE MAN GINNY COULDN'T GET

The boss's luscious wife had every man in the lumberyard eating out of her hand— but Charlie was hip to her little game! . . .

By ALEX AUSTIN

Men
February 1971
"An Invitation From a Nymphomaniac"

True Action
February 1973
"The Man Ginny Couldn't Get"

Stag
August 1963
"Bugsy Siegel, Ever-Lovin' Top Gun of the Syndicate"

Men

August 1969

"The Girl With the Golden Legs"

Stag

August 1966

"Executive Suite Tramp"

Male

April 1970

"Diane's Love Pad"

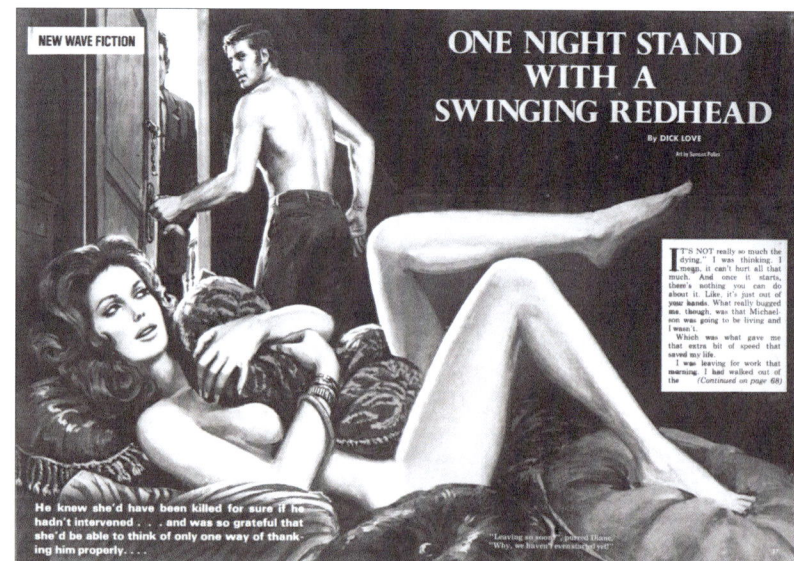

Stag Annual No. 12

September 1972

"One Night Stand With a Swinging Redhead"

Male

October 1963

"You Have 12 Hours to Find Saigon's Nude Taxi-Dancer"

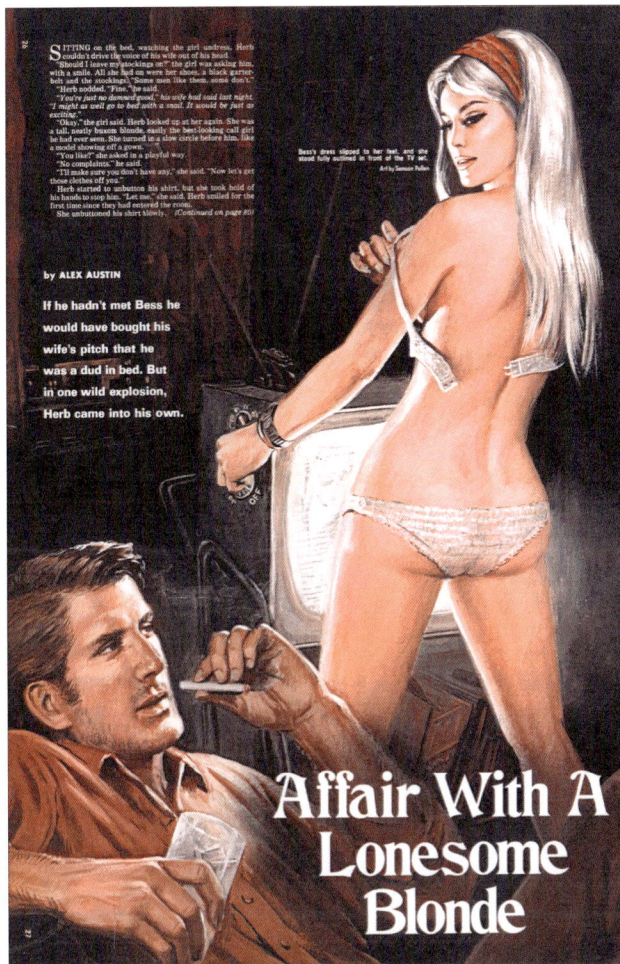

Stag

April 1969

"Affair With a Lonesome Blonde"

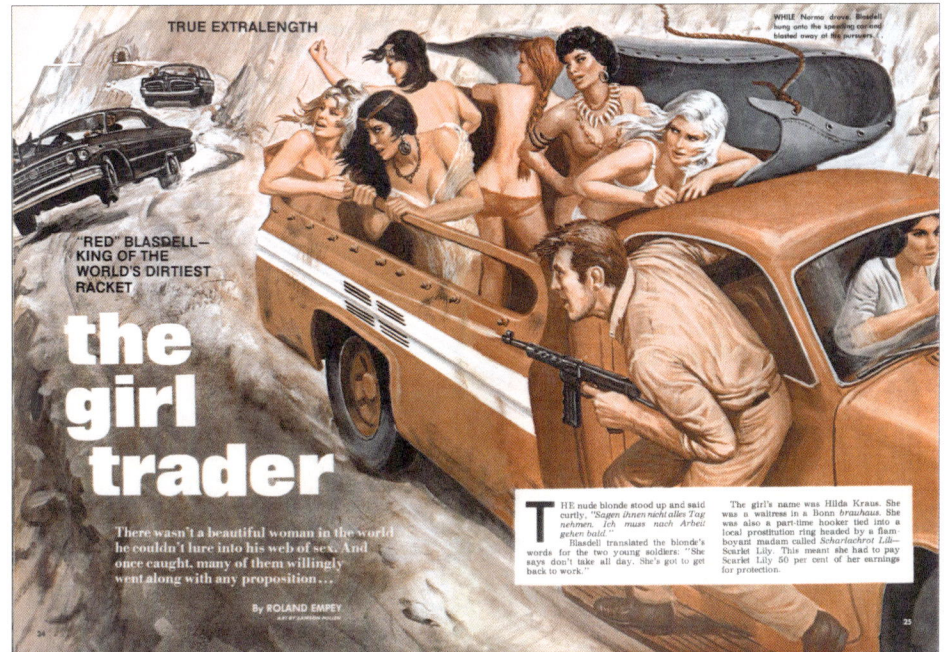

Male

February 1971

"The Girl Trader"

For Men Only
November 1971
"Backwater Woman"

Man's World
August 1968
"Nina and Claire: Ready Every Night"

Stag

June 1965

"'No Limit' Casino Girl"

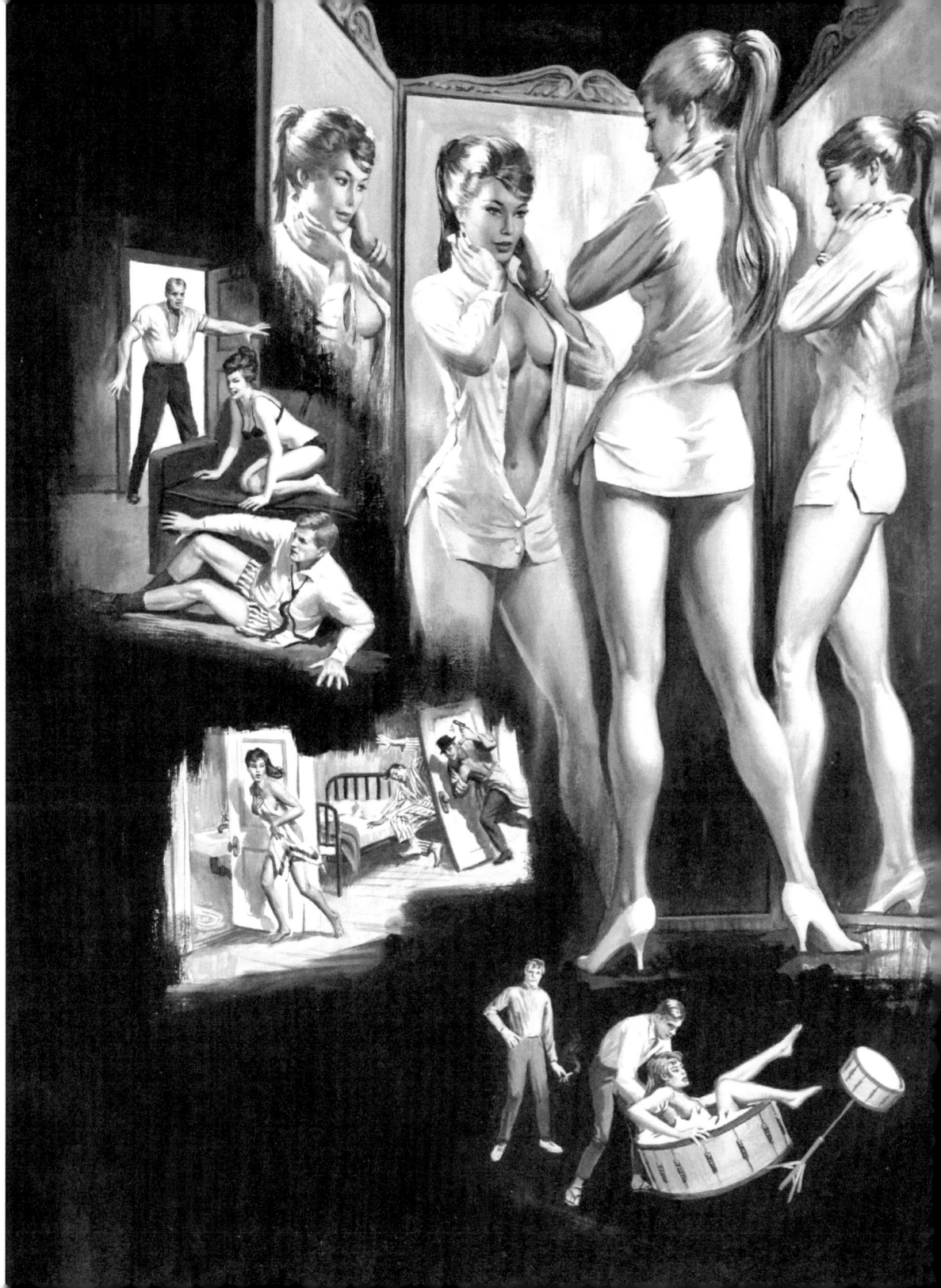

For Men Only
March 1972
"The Love Race"

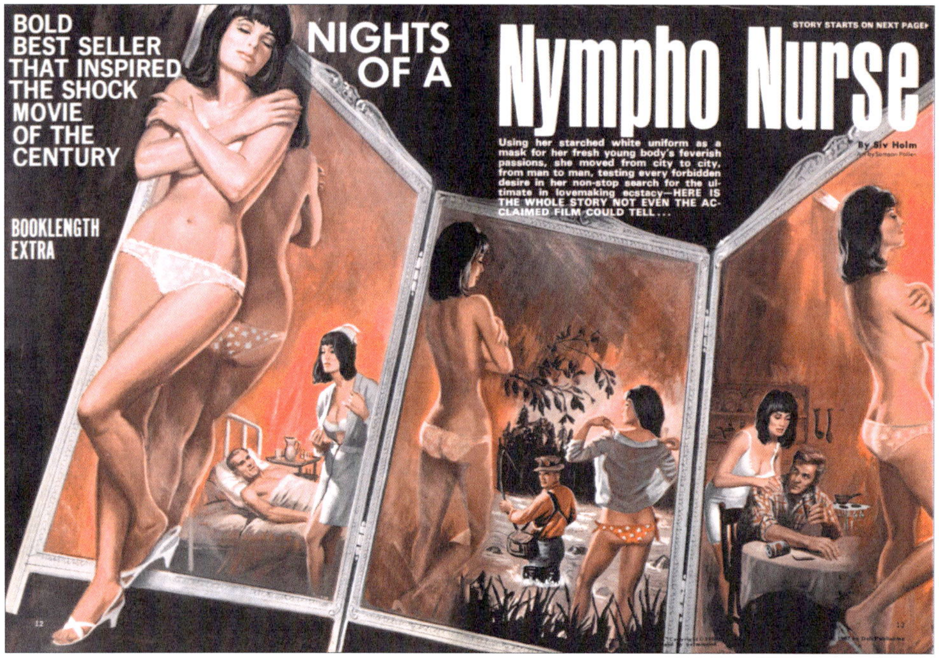

Man's World
February 1968
"Nights of a Nympho Nurse"

Male

June 1967

"Passion Doll on the 23rd Floor"

Male Annual No. 4

1968

"The Blonde Passion Hunter in 507"

Male

April 1968

"Passion Bus Trek"

Male

January 1961

*"The American Corporal and His
'Virgins From Hell' Girls"*

Stag Annual No. 1

1964

"The Five Who Survived 60 Days in Japan's Underground Giant Coffin"

Stag

January 1961

"Vengeance Platoon From the Village of Violated Women"

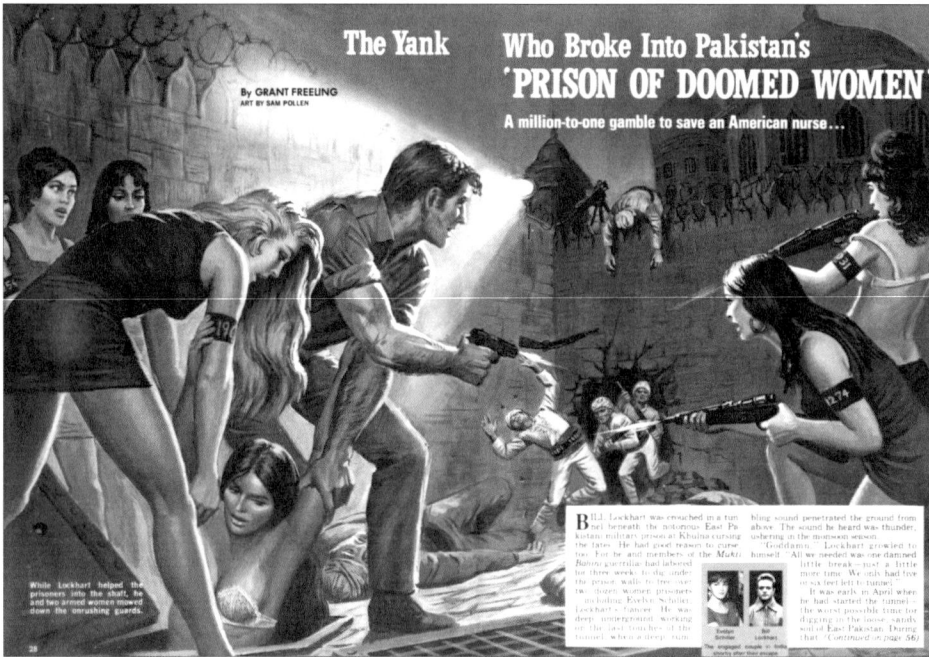

Men
March 1972
*"The Yank Who Broke Into
Pakistan's 'Prison of Doomed Women'"*

Men
December 1966
*"The Dozen Wild Beauties on
Jake Scott's 'Free Love' Island"*

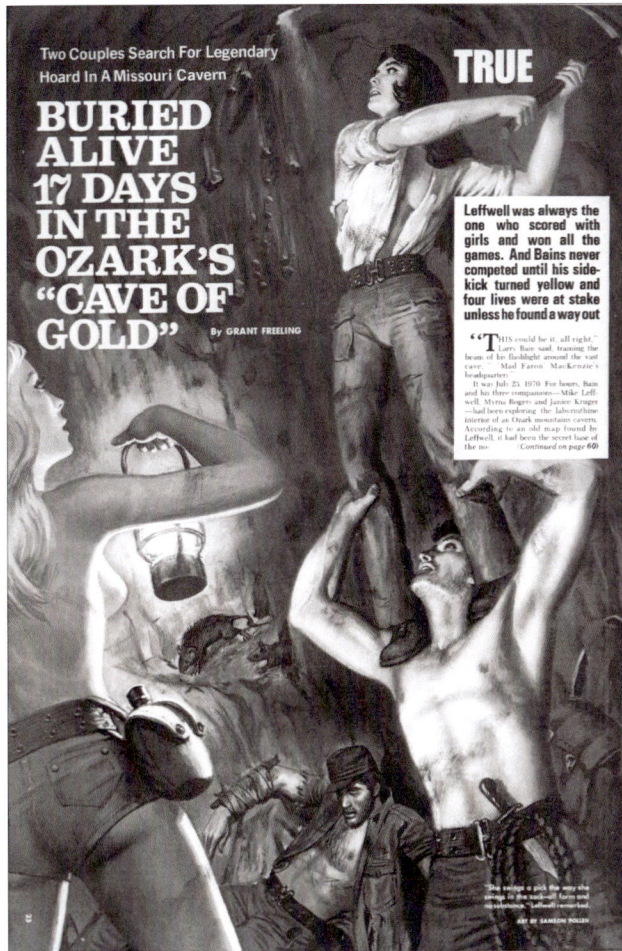

For Men Only

June 1972

"*Buried Alive 17 Days in the Ozark's 'Cave of Gold'*"

Stag

July 1967

"*The Notorious Woman at Beach Camp 40*"

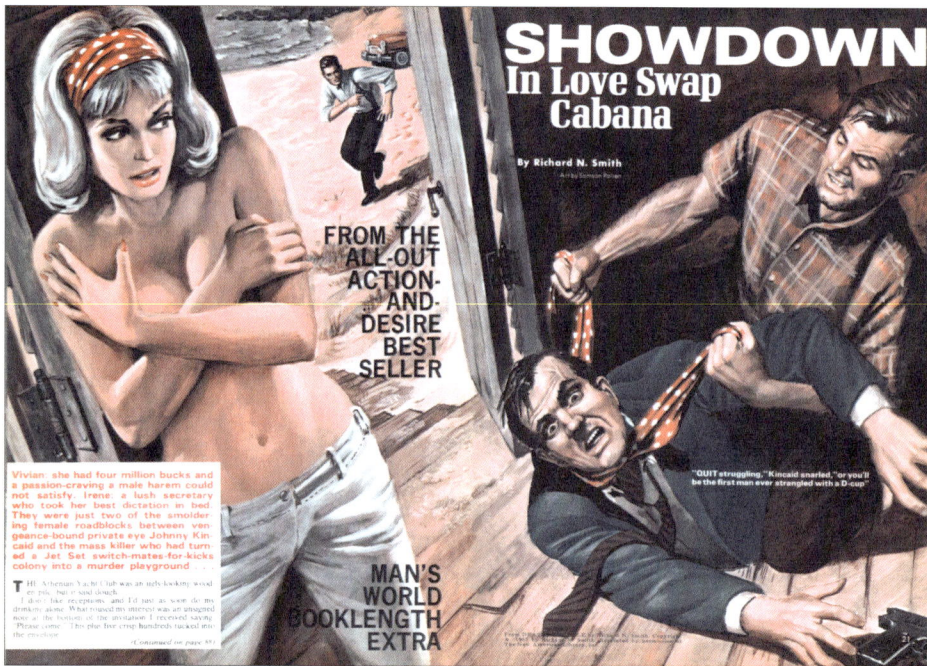

Man's World

August 1967

"Showdown in Love Swap Cabana"

True Action

January 1966

"Madamoiselle Strange Legs"

Male

September 1963

"'Dynamite' Divorcee"

Men

August 1963

*"The Invincible Harvey Stubb, American Hero
Who Wouldn't Stay Dead"*

True Action

January 1969

"Give Me Cycle Love"

For Men Only

October 1966

"Oil Town Tramp"

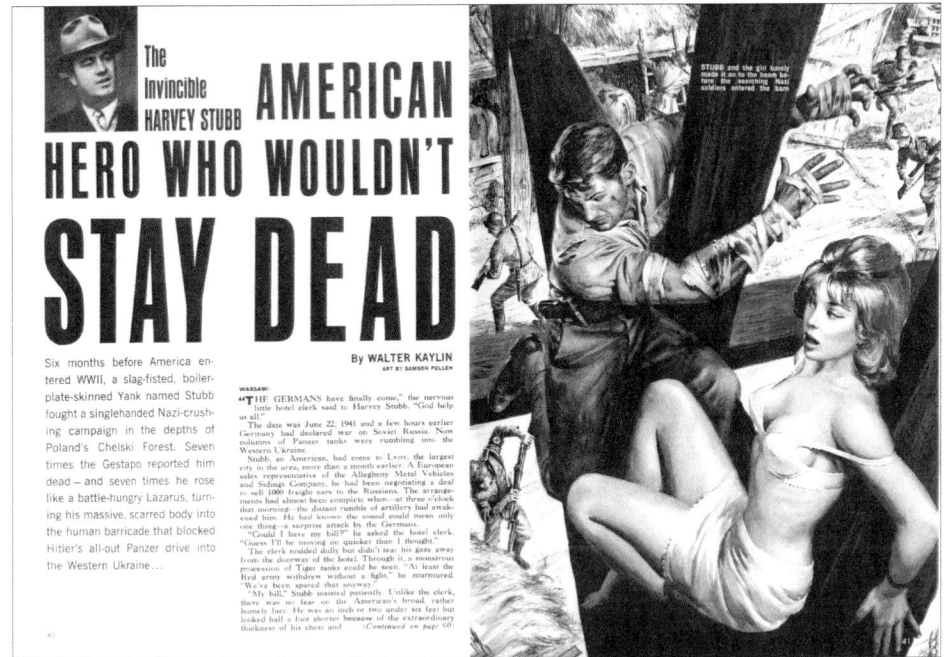

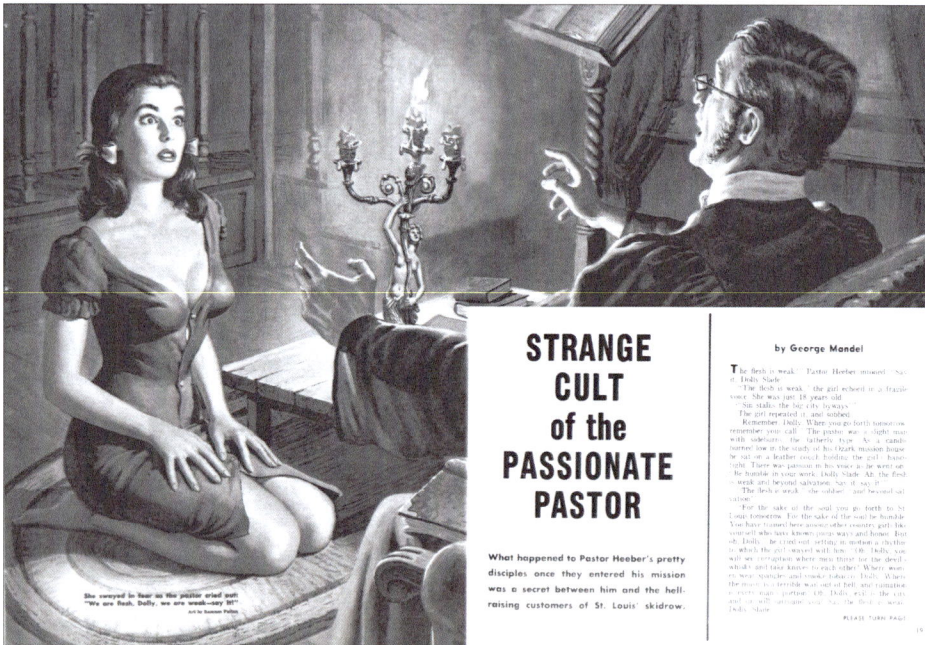

STRANGE
CULT
of the
PASSIONATE
PASTOR

What happened to Pastor Heeber's pretty disciples once they entered his mission was a secret between him and the hell-raising customers of St. Louis' skidrow.

For Men Only
October 1958
"Strange Cult of the Passionate Pastor"

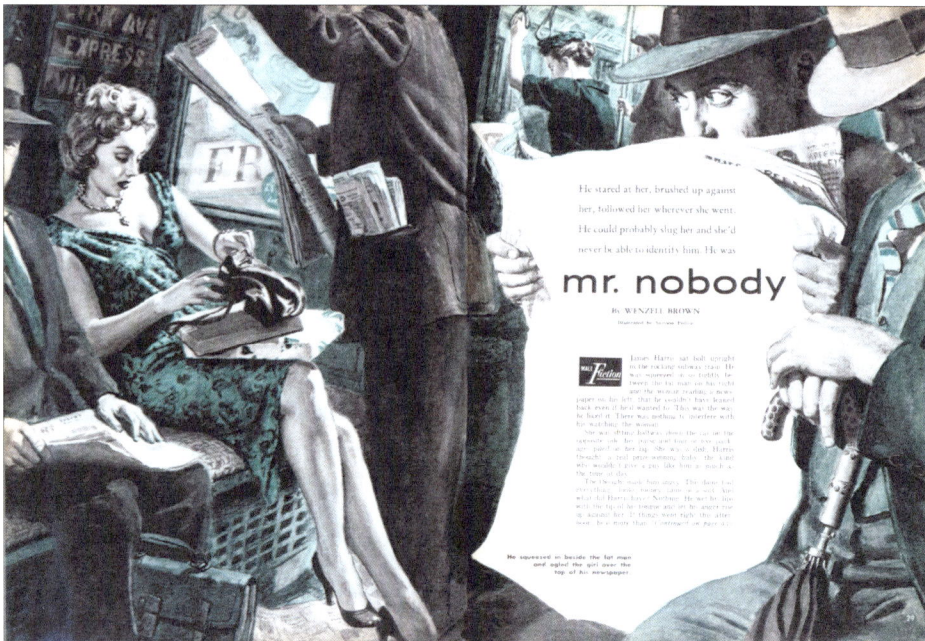

He stared at her, brushed up against her, followed her wherever she went. He could probably slug her and she'd never be able to identify him. He was

mr. nobody

By WENZELL BROWN

Male
February 1957
"Mr. Nobody"

Men

October 1957

"Fun in the Tomb With Dr. Oom"

Stag

August 1958

"The Man Who Hated Streetwalkers"

For Men Only

November 1968

"Date With a Campaign Nymph"

Men

August 1964

"Sure Thing Blonde"

For Men Only

August 1973

"The Green Felt Nymph"

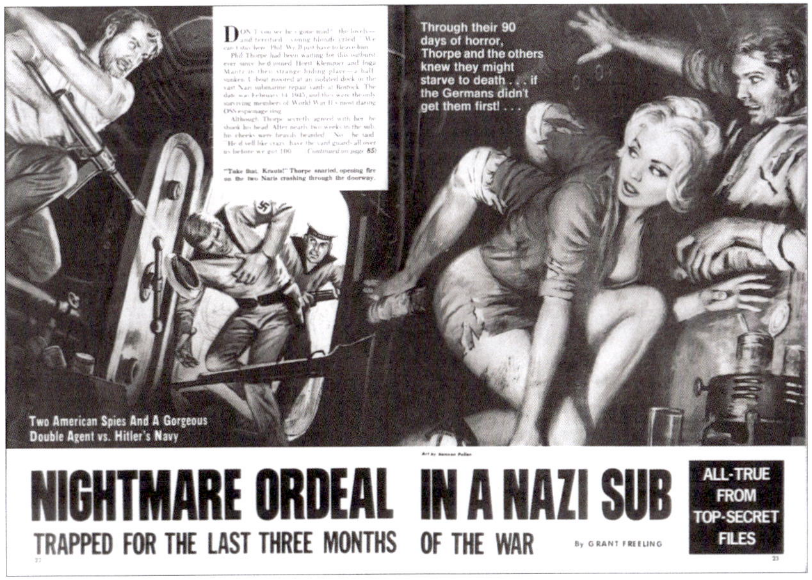

True Action

June 1972

"Nightmare Ordeal in a Nazi Sub"

Male

July 1970

"Trapped 96 Days in a Nazi Sub"

Stag Annual No. 5

1968

"Down Hill Destruction Run of Engine #5"

Men

June 1968

"Ellen Madigan's Love Pad"

Male

April 1964

"Five Greek Girls to Istanbul"

Male

April 1964

"Five Greek Girls to Istanbul"

Men

May 1968

"The Seduction of Wilma"

For Men Only
November 1970
"Locker Room Tease"

Man's World
October 1967
"Entombed 74 Days in 'Naked Virgin' Mine"

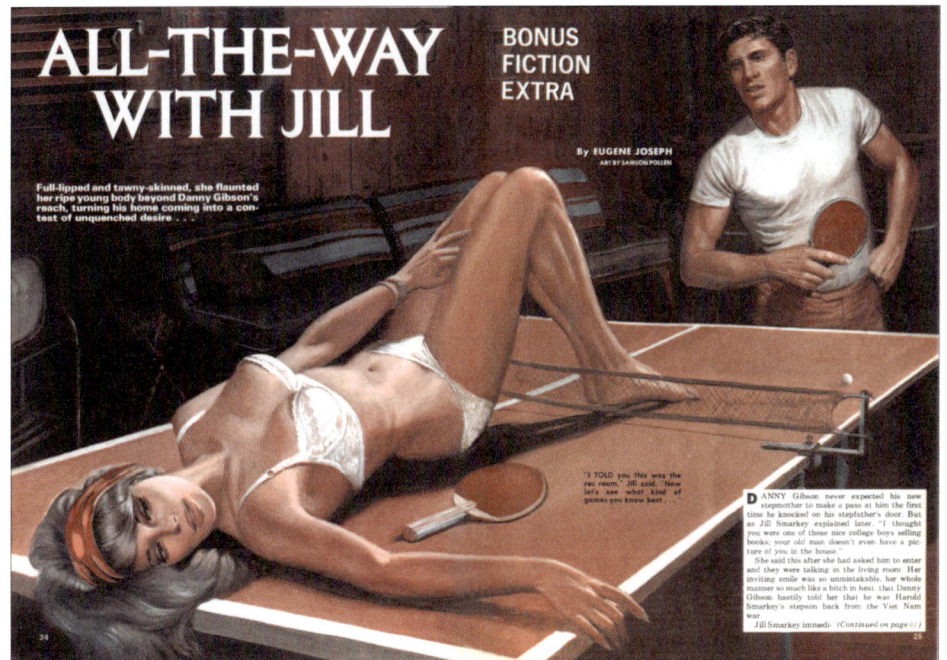

ALL-THE-WAY WITH JILL — BONUS FICTION EXTRA

By EUGENE JOSEPH
ART BY SAMSON POLLEN

Full-lipped and tawny-skinned, she flaunted her ripe young body beyond Danny Gibson's reach, turning his home coming into a contest of unquenched desire . . .

"I TOLD you this was the rec room," Jill said. "Now let's see what kind of games you know best."

DANNY GIBSON never expected his new stepmother to make a pass at him the first time he knocked on his stepfather's door. But as Jill Smarkey explained later: "I thought you were one of those nice college boys selling books; your old man doesn't even have a picture of you in the house."

She said this after she had asked him to enter and they were talking in the living room. Her inviting smile was so unmistakable, her whole manner so much like a bitch in heat, that Danny Gibson hastily told her that he was Harold Smarkey's stepson back from the Viet Nam war.

Jill Smarkey immedi- *(Continued on page 87)*

Male

July 1968

"All-the-Way With Jill"

A man had to crawl to her, then worship her body in every way she commanded. But once he reached that stage she was already planning his replacement

She jerked the wheel against her naked flesh, grinning as he flipped backwards into the sea.

by ALEX AUSTIN

EXTRALENGTH

COME TO MY BED

STORY STARTS NEXT PAGE

Male Annual No. 6

1968

"Come to My Bed"

Male

February 1972

"Shack Woman"

For Men Only

May 1971

"Della Rose, The Sheriff's Not So Virgin Daughter"

Stag

January 1972

"The FBI and the Great Mob Double-Cross"

For Men Only

November 1969

"The Runaway Lover"

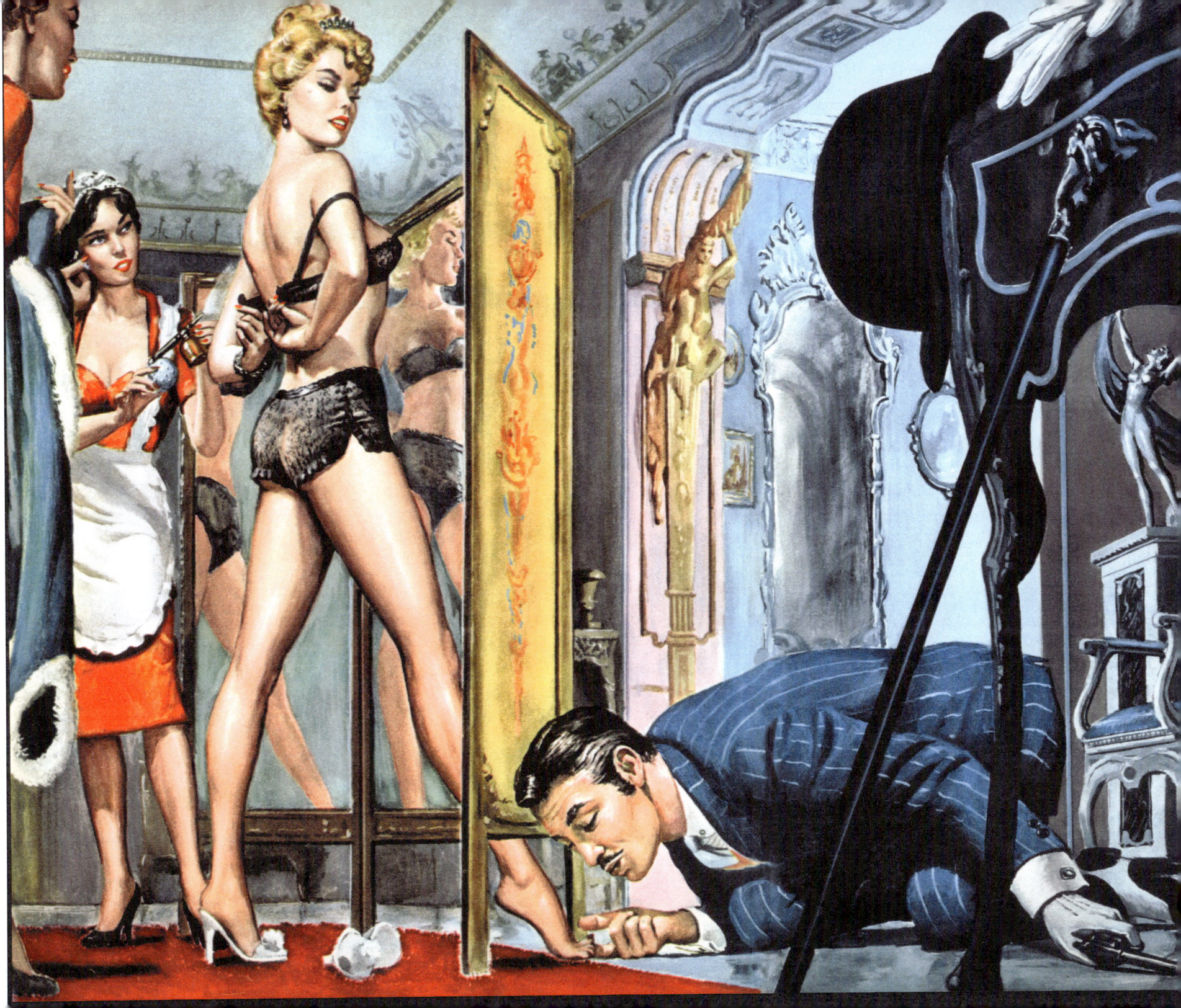

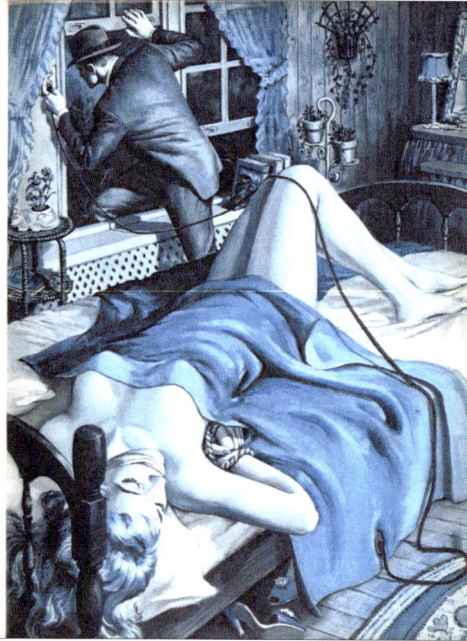

Men

October 1959

"The Blonde Who Got a Charge Out of Death"

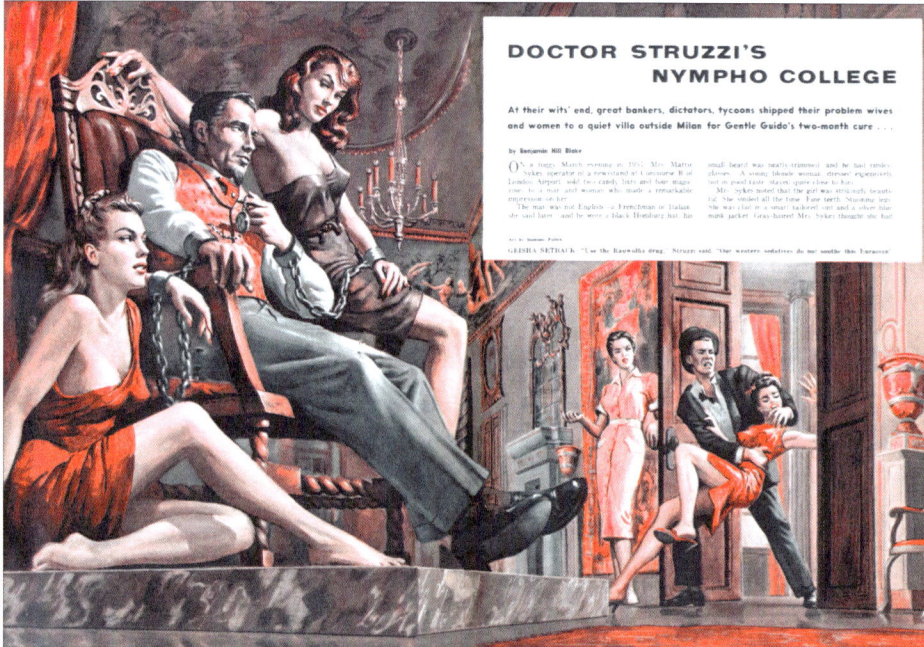

Men

September 1959

"Doctor Struzzi's Nympho College"

Stag

August 1960

"Trackdown of Hitler's Floating Love Camp"

Men

January 1960

"Girl With the Sweet Pink Toes"

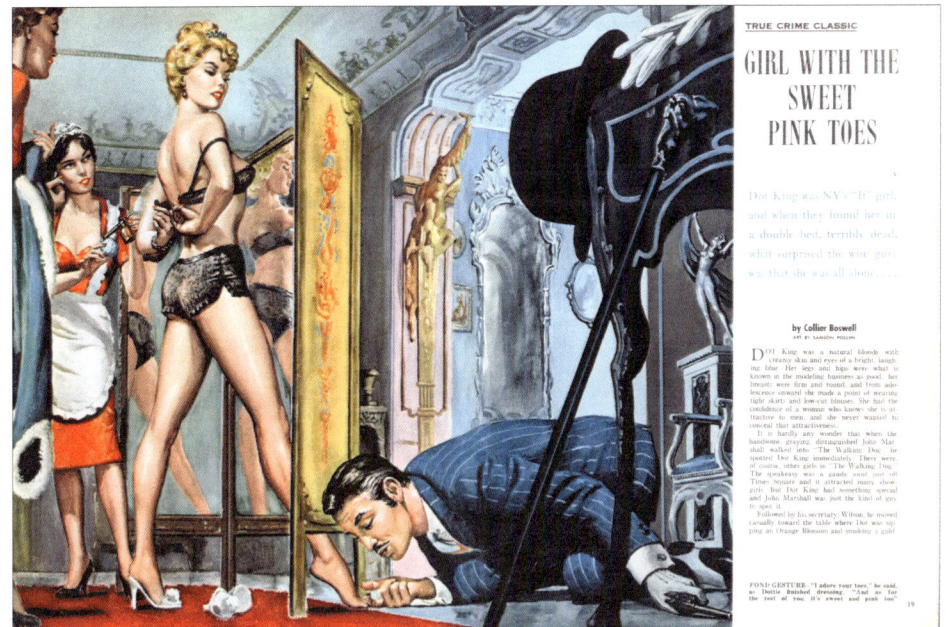

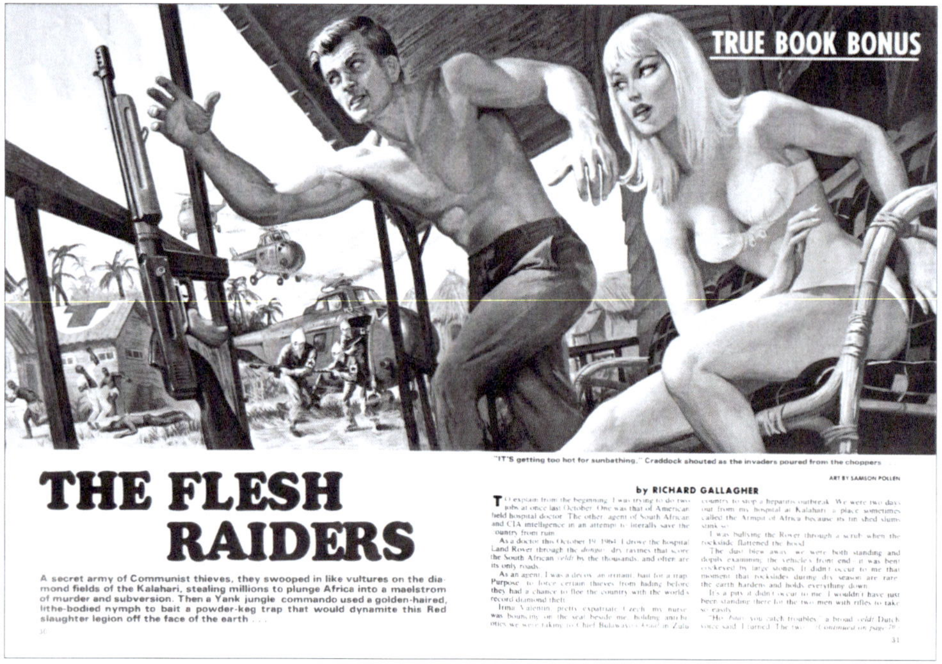

True Action
July 1967
"The Flesh Raiders"

Stag
November 1962
"Penal Queen of Capt. 'Crazy's' Jungle Terror Colony"

Action Life

November 1964

"'Shipwreck' Cameron's Castaway Love Colony"

Male

December 1969

"General Hooker's Woman"

The Scandal That Fired Virginia City

HARVEY CRITTENDEN'S IMPATIENT MISTRESS

THE HUSHED-UP SCANDAL OF RUSSIA'S SIN STOCKADES

Forcing their prostitutes, extortionists, B-girls and teenage jailbait into Siberian compounds for "rehabilitation," the Reds have unwittingly set up vice cities of frustrated females, primed to explode with man-hungry fury

STORY STARTS ON PAGE 37

EXCLUSIVE
INSIDE A COMMUNIST ALL-WOMAN PENAL CAMP

Male
July 1959
"Harvey Crittenden's Impatient Mistress"

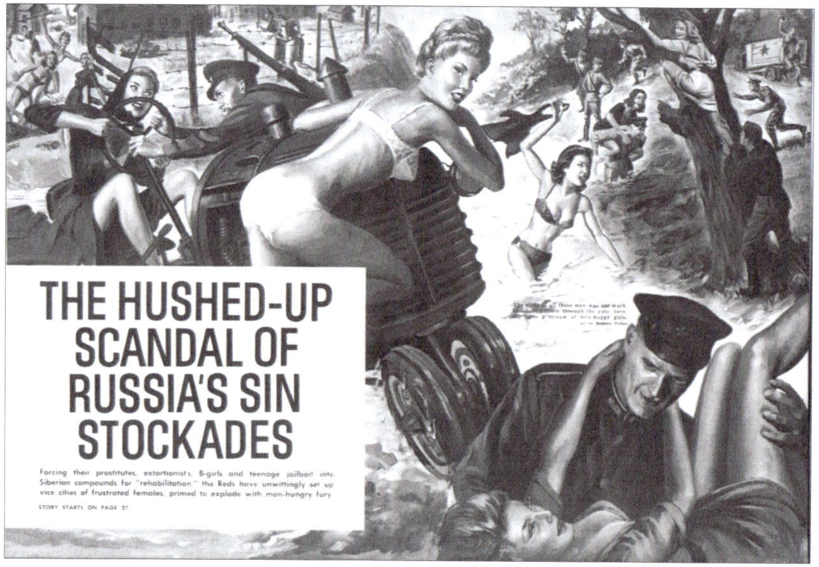

Action For Men
September 1966
"The Hushed-Up Scandal of Russia's Sin Stockades"

Stag
January 1964
"Inside a Communist All-Woman Penal Camp"

130

Male

September 1960

*"The Caribbean Kingdom of
Six-Foot Sarah Glad"*

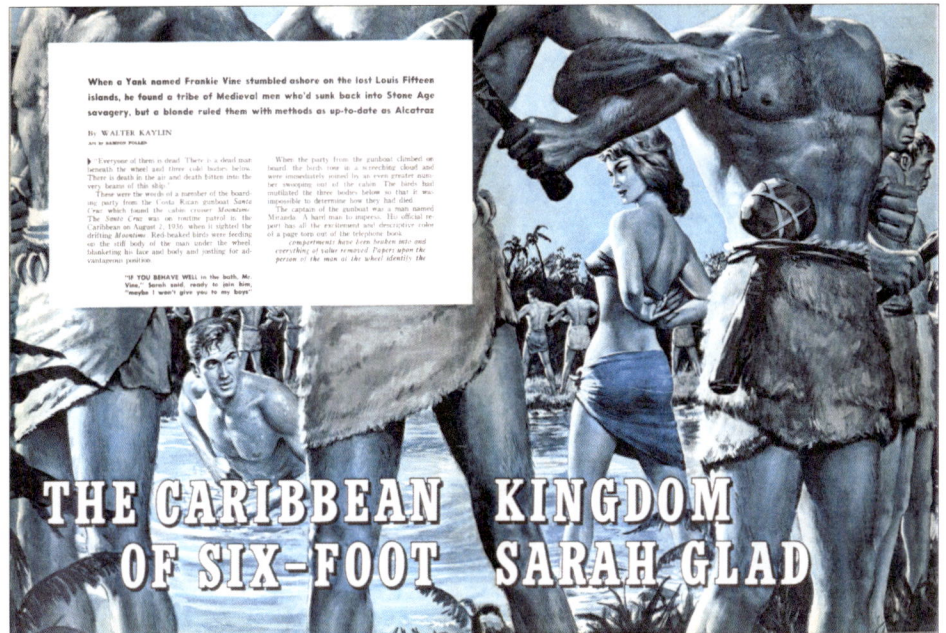

Stag

January 1960

*"World War II's Forgotten Sailor and
His Desert Shangri-La"*

Men
July 1958
"Herr Doktor Gross' Shocking Fraulein Camps"

"I painted the type of woman that was the style at the time, whether it was Marilyn Monroe if the character was a blonde, or a nice looking brunette like Audrey Hepburn...whatever was fashionable. Instinctively. Not really thinking it out that much—I lean towards that approach. Sometimes they look like famous actresses just because I use good features: a cute nose, big eyes, a nice shape to the face and body...and then when it was all done, it looked like somebody. But it wasn't intended to look like somebody. I did a couple where they said, 'Oh, that's Marilyn Monroe.' It wasn't Marilyn Monroe. It's just that I drew the model in a way that didn't look

THE CASE OF THE
DEADLY DOLL

Blonde and beautiful Anna Marie knocked off more
of Cincinnati's senior citizens than a flu epidemic. She
found 'em, fooled 'em, married 'em—and then stuffed
the old duffers with enough arsenic to kill a horse.
Here's the astonishing story of a truly deadly doll

by CHARLES HENRY, JR.
ILLUSTRATED BY SAMPSON POLLEN

Old Jake was having the time of his life with Anna and became as frisky as a yearling goat—until she cooked for him.

Adventure
April 1959
"The Case of the Deadly Doll"

like the reference photographs, didn't look like the model that I used. But she ended up looking like Marilyn Monroe, because I used the kind of features Marilyn Monroe had. It was a coincidence. I got a lot out of that method, putting in what was pretty at the time, good features. So they ended up looking like movie stars or whatever. And their shape, you know, I'd build it up a little bit.... Sometimes the movie star's not perfect, either. They're only human."

135

Pollen's
ACTION

THE ART OF SAMSON POLLEN   EDITED BY ROBERT DEIS & WYATT DOYLE

Pollen IN PRINT

1955-1959

THE ART OF SAMSON POLLEN

EDITED BY **ROBERT DEIS & WYATT DOYLE**

THE MEN'S ADVENTURE LIBRARY

MANY TITLES AVAILABLE IN SOFTCOVER, EBOOK, AND DELUXE EXPANDED HARDCOVER EDITIONS

ROBERT DEIS AND WYATT DOYLE, SERIES EDITORS

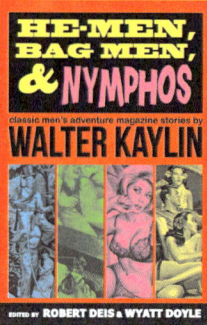

He-Men, Bag Men, & Nymphos
Stories by Walter Kaylin

Leaving an indelible mark on three decades of sweat-soaked pulp fiction, Walter Kaylin tackled testosterone-fueled subjects from Westerns to war, secret agents to sex sirens, Nazis to noir. His frequently over-the-top plots and characters scaled new heights of ingenuity and invention, while setting the standard for the kind of unapologetic savagery and excess that made men's adventure magazines notorious, then and now. Includes reminiscences by Kaylin, his family, and his former editor, writer Bruce Jay Friedman.

Atomic Werewolves and Man-Eating Plants: When MAMs Got Weird

Featuring Theodore Sturgeon, Manly Wade Wellman, Gardner Francis Fox, Gil Paust, Rick Rubin, HP Lovecraft, *and more*

Weird MAM tales of supernatural encounters, monstrous cryptids, vampirism, witchcraft, demonic death cults, killer robots, psychotic chicken butchers, and of course, atomic werewolves and man-eating plants!

"Hands down, one of my favorite books of 2023."
—Stephen Bissette (*Swamp Thing, Tyrant*)

Recommended by The Washington Post

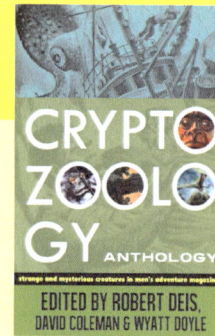

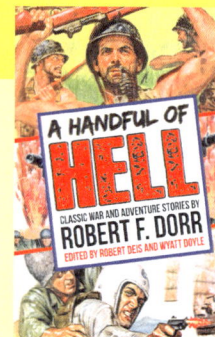

Cryptozoology Anthology
With guest editor David Coleman
Featuring Arthur C. Clarke, John Keel *and others*

When American men had questions about the Yeti, the Loch Ness Monster, Bigfoot, and other weird beasts from the strange world of cryptozoology, they found answers in the hard-hitting pages of men's adventure magazines. Here are samples of sensational period reporting and wild, "true" accounts of savage, fist-to-claw duels between man and Sasquatch, man and fishman, man and monster! Plus expert analysis by crypto authority **David Coleman**, cryptid-by-cryptid commentary, and much, much more. Don't leave civilization without it!

Recommended by The Washington Post

A Handful of Hell
Stories by Robert F. Dorr

Aviator, diplomat, and historian, Robert F. Dorr was uniquely qualified to write for men's adventure magazines, bringing sweat-and-blood, nuts-and-bolts authenticity to his stories of risk, combat, and sacrifice. Vivid, gripping tales of aerial conflict, battlefield heroism and action—some fact, some fiction, all adrenaline-fueled, white-knuckle adventure from one of the genre's greatest voices.

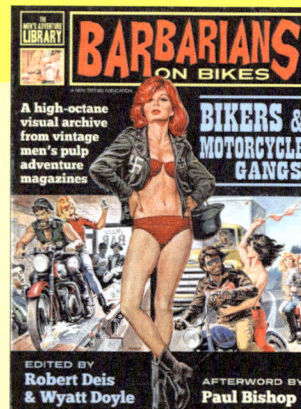

Barbarians on Bikes
Afterword by Paul Bishop

An oversized color collection compiling three decades of motorcycle-themed magazine covers and interior spreads from the 1950s through the 1970s, most unseen since their original publication. Biker illustration art at its most savage. A biker movie between covers, **Barbarians on Bikes** is big, bad, and untamed… Think you can handle the ride?

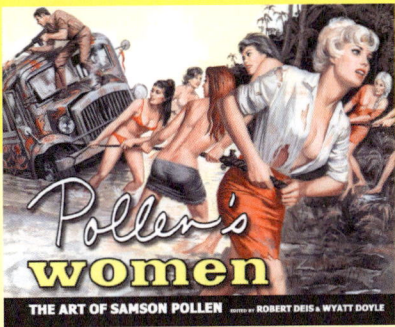

THE ART OF SAMSON POLLEN
Pollen's Women
Pollen's Action
Pollen in Print 1955–1959

A series of lush visual archives collecting some of artist Samson Pollen's most memorable pieces, selected from the hundreds of jaw-dropping illustrations he provided for men's adventure magazines (MAMs) from the 1950s through the 1970s. Pollen was equally celebrated for his abilities to effectively render action and movement, as well as his gift for painting beautiful and dangerous women. Illustrating work from authors like Mario Puzo, Martin Cruz Smith, Richard Stark (Donald Westlake), Norman Mailer, Ed McBain, Richard Wright, Don Pendleton, Erskine Caldwell, Walter Kaylin, and Robert F. Dorr, Pollen's immersive illustrations transported adventure-hungry readers from tropical jungles to brutal battlefields to raging seas and mean city streets. Samson Pollen painted it all—spectacularly. Yet almost none of these stunning illustrations have seen print since their original publication. Until now.

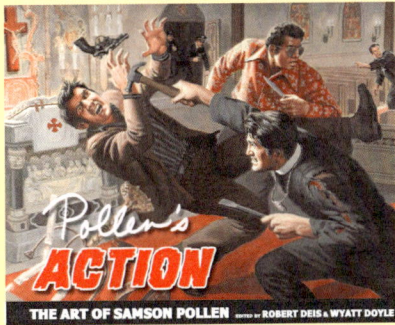

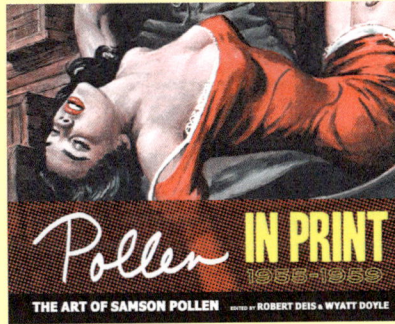

Both **Pollen's Women** and **Pollen's Action** are drawn from the artist's own exhaustive archives of his original artwork for MAMs, while **Pollen in Print 1955–1959** is the inaugural volume of a projected series presenting his artwork chronologically as it appeared in the magazines, allowing us to fill gaps in Pollen's archive and definitively chart the trajectory of a remarkable career.

All three big 11" x 8.5" horizontal volumes include the late artist's reminiscences and autobiographical comments.

Eva: Men's Adventure Supermodel
by Eva Lynd

Blonde Swedish countess Eva Lynd's multi-faceted career touches every aspect of 20th century popular culture. A model for leading illustration artists and top glamour and pin-up photographers of the era, she also appeared with some of the biggest names in entertainment on both the big and small screens. Eva shares her story in her own words and pictures. Includes artwork from pulp masters such as Norm Eastman, Al Rossi, Mike Ludlow, and James Bama.

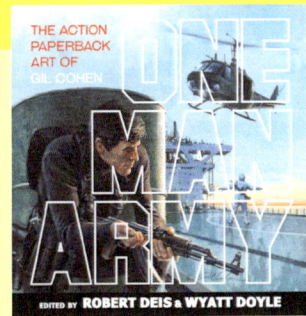

One Man Army *by* Gil Cohen

Exploring the incomparable talent of Gil Cohen via the unique perspective he brought to the Mack Bolan universe as one of **The Executioner** series' most celebrated cover artists. **One Man Army** showcases Cohen's spectacular and original paintings for the bestselling action paperbacks, chronicling his seminal role in establishing the Bolan mythos for millions of dedicated readers worldwide.

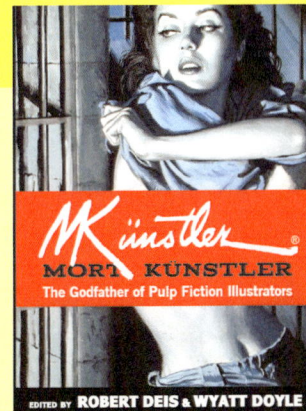

Mort Künstler: The Godfather of Pulp Fiction Illustrators

Celebrated for his ability to present large-scale action while never losing sight of essential details, **Mort Künstler** is a master of capturing conflict in paint—both its spectacle, and human cost. At last, here is a stunning selection of his finest pieces from the MAM era in this long awaited collection. A close study of an unequaled career, every page explodes with action, color, and artistry.

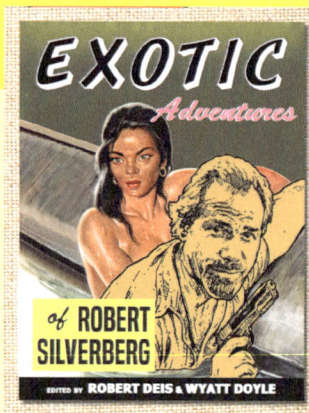

Exotic Adventures of Robert Silverberg

From safari to bordello, from smugglers' cove to opium den, Robert Silverberg's lost pulp exotica returns to print for the first time since its original 1950s publication, presented in bold new facsimile re-creations that look fresh off the newsstand, circa 1958. Strap in for fully illustrated globe-trotting adventures from the vivid imagination of one of speculative fiction's most honored talents, working incognito.

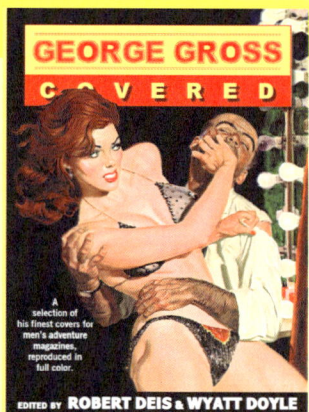

George Gross: Covered

A top artist for pulps, men's adventure magazines, and paperback covers, George Gross's artwork spans decades, and helped establish a visual vocabulary for action/adventure and hard-boiled fiction. A unique talent who led the way for generations of artists, his imagery continues to inspire and influence. Spotlighting dozens of his memorable covers, this full-color collection includes contributions by historian David Saunders and artist Mort Künstler.

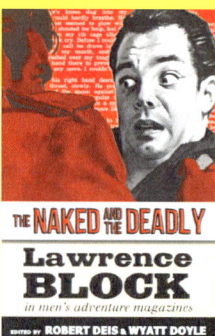

The Naked and the Deadly
Stories by Lawrence Block

Spicy detective stories, international intrigue, and bedroom secrets… Before the bestsellers, Block cut his teeth on MAM fiction and nonfiction articles, collected here in their complete and uncut versions for the first time since their original publication. Includes a new introduction by the author.

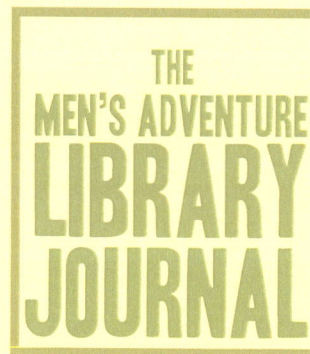

THE MEN'S ADVENTURE LIBRARY JOURNAL

SOFTCOVER AND EXPANDED HARDCOVER EDITIONS AVAILABLE

ROBERT DEIS AND WYATT DOYLE, SERIES EDITORS

I Watched Them Eat Me Alive
Killer Creatures in Men's Adventure Magazines

Cuba: Sugar, Sez, and Slaughter
Cuba and Castro in Men's Adventure Magazines

Maneaters
Killer Sharks in Men's Adventure Magazines

The Men's Adventure Library Journal is a bold and explosive annex of The Men's Adventure Library, devoted to deep dives into some of MAMs' most popular and potent subjects. Titles include I Watched Them Eat Me Alive, a hot appetizer sampler of killer creature survival stories; Cuba: Sugar, Sex, and Slaughter, presenting MAM fact and fiction centered on Castro and the Cuba in the 1960s; and Maneaters, a savage collection of terrifying shark fiction and illustration art paired with mythbusting by contemporary shark experts, including contributions by Shark Week creator Steve Cheskin and sharkfilm director Ace Hannah. All are available in softcover and expanded hardcover editions featuring additional content.

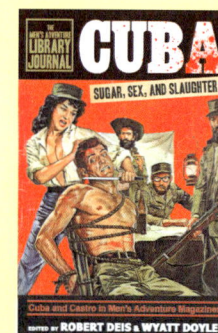

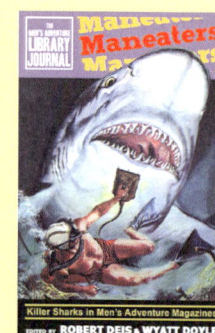

By Jimmy Angelina & Wyatt Doyle

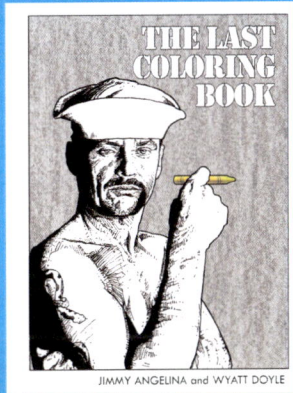

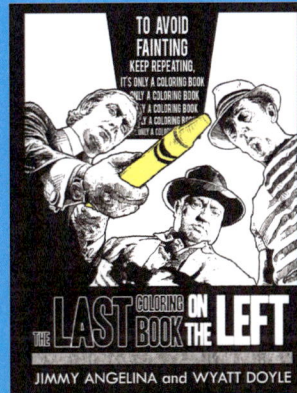

The Last Coloring Book
The Last Coloring Book on the Left

"Images of great movie icons, groundbreakers, and cult movie weirdos…in a pair of VERY unusual works of cinephilia. These are 'anti-coloring books' populated by cult heroes and heroines…"
—Ed Grant, *Media Funhouse*

"Truly inspired!" —Steven Puchalski, *Shock Cinema*

"Perfect gifts for the cult movie fan. Crayons not included."
—Laura Wagner, *Classic Images*

Be Italian

People pretending to be Italian and Italians pretending not to be. A one-of-a-kind visual history exploring Italian identity in motion pictures from the silent era 'til now. Featured on *Gilbert Gottfried's Amazing Colossal Podcast.*

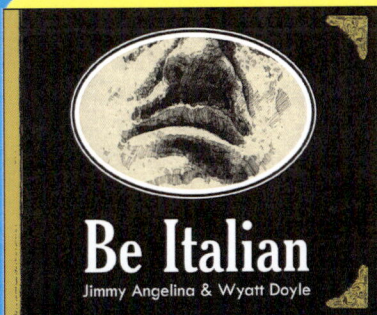

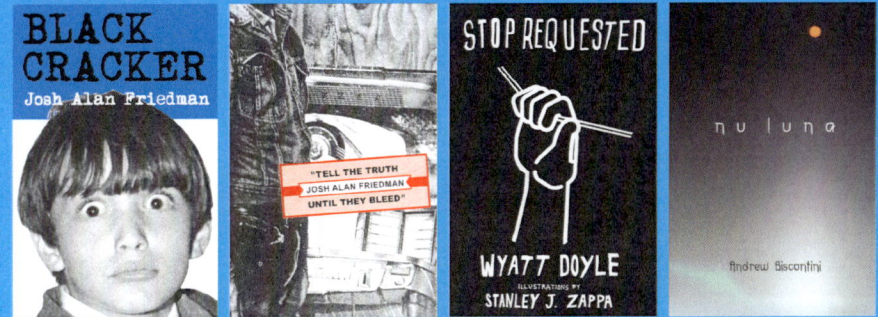

Black Cracker, *an autobiographical novel by* Josh Alan Friedman

1962, flashpoint of the civil rights struggle. And young Josh is the lone white boy in a segregated grade school. An unflinching fun-house tour of a Long Island boyhood, and its now-forgotten poor Black shantytowns. Hilarious and heartbreaking.

Tell the Truth Until They Bleed, *by* Josh Alan Friedman

Up close and personal with important and unsung figures in blues and rock 'n' roll: the self-made, the self-serving, and the self-destructive. Illuminating parts of the music industry most don't talk about, this is show business without the showbiz.

Stop Requested, *stories by* Wyatt Doyle; *illus.* Stanley J. Zappa

"A series of rueful, witty and occasionally heartwrenching stories about riding the bus in LA. Doyle finds consequence in the inconsequential. He's Bukowski without the nasty streak. And he's real good. Highly recommended." —Marc Campbell, *Dangerous Minds*

nu luna, *a novel by* Andrew Biscontini

After 400 years of colonization, the moon is home to nearly a billion people, living in a crowded industrial police state on the verge of collapse. *nu luna* is a deeply personal matinee space adventure, spun through an improbably plausible future history. The future is beautiful and dangerous.

AVAILABLE IN SOFTCOVER AND DELUXE HARDCOVER WITH ADDITIONAL CONTENT

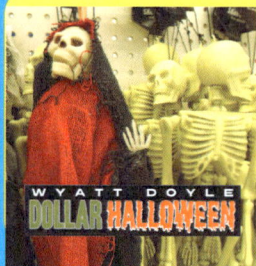

Dollar Halloween

Documenting off-brand junk and sparkly death totems, made to be thrown away. Where there's a need, or even a mild desire, a dollar store stands ready to fill it for whatever you've got in your pocket.

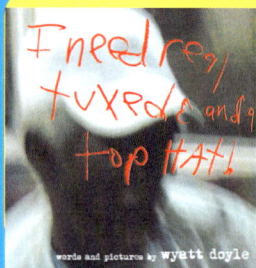

I Need Real Tuxedo and a Top Hat!

On the buses, on the corners, in the city streets. Portraits and lives of the forgotten, the avoided, the ignored. Street people and street life in raw, poignant photographs and stories.

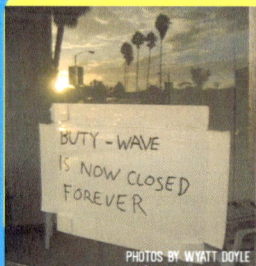

Buty-Wave Is Now Closed Forever

Things that are gone, and things that remain. Includes portraits of Rev. Raymond Branch, Georgina Spelvin, Ray Bradbury, George Clayton Johnson, Tura Satana, Ernest Borgnine, and Carl Ballantine.

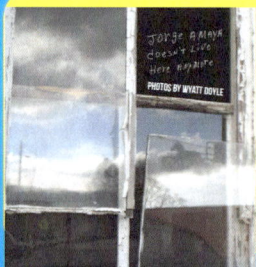

Jorge Amaya Doesn't Live Here Anymore

Abandoned places, empty spaces, forgotten faces. Indelible images from across the United States, documenting the wreckage and remnants of the American experience after the parade has passed.

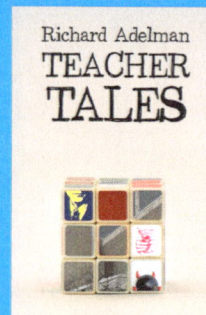

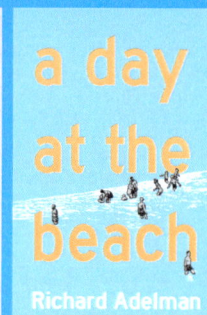

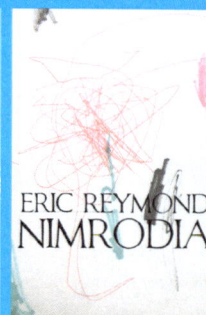

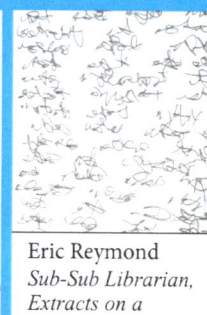

@photobywyattdoyle

Teacher Tales, *a novel by* Richard Adelman

For 40 years, Mr. Kessler has kept his head down and not made waves. But new acquaintances and bad decisions in his final year before retirement bring his ordered world crashing down around him—tragically and hysterically. A smart and darkly comic novel.

A Day at the Beach, *a novel by* Richard Adelman

Atlantic City, summer of '63. A boy. A girl. And the other boy, who reluctantly pretends to date her to help his pal. A funny, nostalgic novel of young love, best friends, and poetry, capturing one 12-year-old's last great summer as a kid down the shore.

Nimrodia, *poems by* Eric Reymond

Visual art and ancient history are the starting point for most of the poems in this collection, as the modern world intersects with these domains again and again. Though language, culture, and time may divide us, these are also the forces that link us together.

Sub-Sub Librarian, Extracts on a, *poems by* Eric Reymond

The title poem imagines *Moby Dick*'s Sub-Sub Librarian experiencing transcendence and illumination through his wide readings. Additional poems find inspiration in texts as diverse as contemporary poetry, vocabulary quizzes, and course syllabi.

Things That Were Made for Love: The Songsheet Art of Sydney Leff

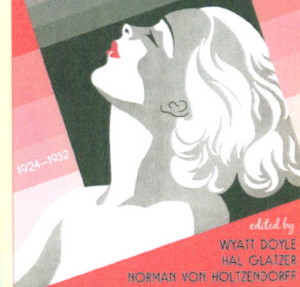

Wyatt Doyle, Hal Glatzer, Norman von Holtzendorff, *editors*

The first-ever songsheet art collection presenting the cream of the Jazz Age illustration artist's work on songsheet covers from 1924–1932. A gorgeous visual feast that playfully captures the moods, elegance, and style of an era.

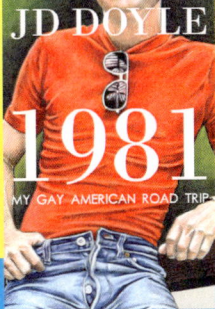

1981—My Gay American Road Trip

by JD Doyle

A playful, intimate, one-of-a-kind illustrated record of gay life, love, lust, and liberation post-Stonewall, in the heady days before the devastating crisis that would change everything.

#new texture Music

CD / DOWNLOAD

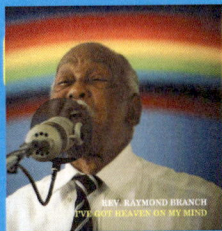

I've Got Heaven on My Mind
Reverend Raymond Branch

Sixty Goddammit Josh Alan

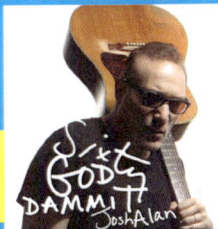

Jimmy Angelina s/t

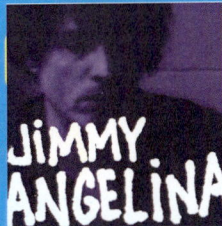

Cursed Carolina

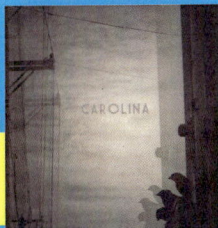

Continental / International
Jon E. Edwards

Map of the Moon s/t

Sing-Song Songs
Stanley J. Zappa

Free / Refuse
Hall, Skrowaczewski, Zappa

Live a Little
Manzappaczewski

The Stanley J. Zappa Quartet
Plays for The Society of Women Engineers

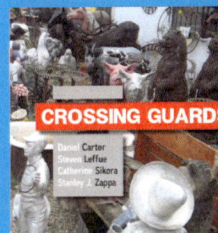

Crossing Guards
Carter, Leffue, Sikora, Zappa

Turkey Bacon Donuts Bitches
MANZAP REBORN

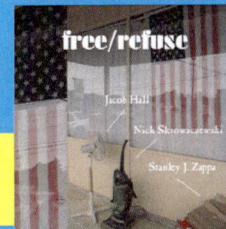

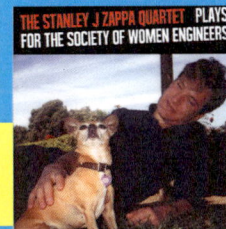

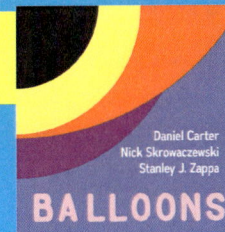

Balloons
Daniel Carter, Nick Skrowaczewski, Stanley J. Zappa

#new texture Words and Pictures and Music

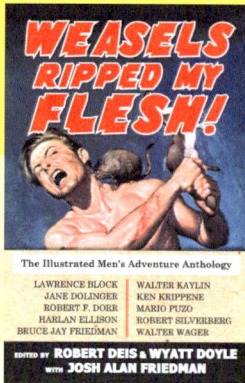

Weasels Ripped My Flesh! *(revised and expanded color edition)*
With guest editor Josh Alan Friedman
Featuring Lawrence Block, Robert F. Dorr, Harlan Ellison, Bruce Jay Friedman, Walter Kaylin, Mario Puzo, Robert Silverberg *and more.*

From the jungles to the deserts to the mean city streets, the men's adventure magazines of the 1950s, '60s and '70s left no male fantasy or interest unexplored. War stories, exotic adventure yarns, (allegedly) true, first-hand accounts of white-knuckle clashes between man and beast, and spicy tales of sadistic frauleins and tropical queens hungry for companionship…plus salacious exposés of then-shocking subjects like free love, the Beat Generation, LSD, homosexuality, and the secret horniness hidden in calypso lyrics. This definitive guide to MAM fiction is your passport to a gonzo world where manly men fought small mammals bare-handed!

Recommended by The Washington Post

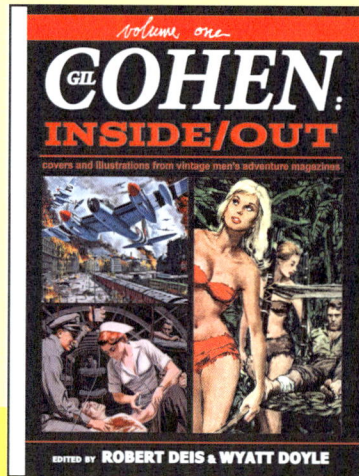

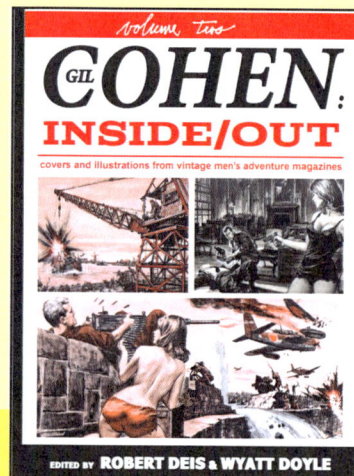

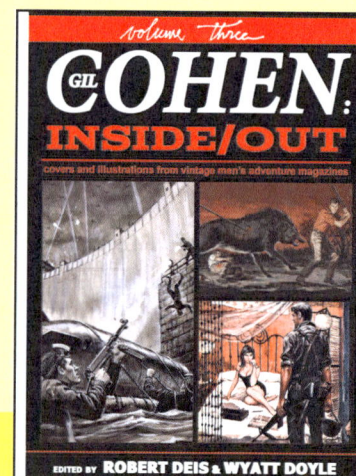

Gil Cohen: Inside/Out, Volumes 1–3

Presenting Gil Cohen's earliest published pieces, as an illustrator and cover artist for men's adventure magazines (MAMs). Cohen created memorable illustrations for just about every kind of story MAMs published: military battles on land, sea, and, of course, air; exotic adventures; hard-boiled crime; historical action; animal attacks; biker, Nazi, and Communist villainy; sexy potboilers and more. This stunning body of work represents both the longest and, until now, least revisited period of his career—almost all of it unseen and unreprinted since their original publication. The series pairs print versions of Cohen's MAM illustrations with their original artwork, and includes the Artist's reminiscences and commentary.

All Roads Lead to Great Neck, *by* Josh Alan Friedman

Sacred hash pipes, high school freakouts, and the brief, intoxicated life of Bruce Disoto, a doomed adolescent hippie in 1970 who sees visions of a 19th century Jewish pimp while tripping. Welcome to psychedelic Great Neck.

"Equal parts Portnoy's Complaint, Catch-22, The Mysteries of Pittsburgh, *and* A Mother's Kisses, *with a dose of magic realism and mucho drugs—plus a lot more than the sum of these parts: a laugh-out-loud dystopian hipster* bildungsroman *with a heart of gold."*

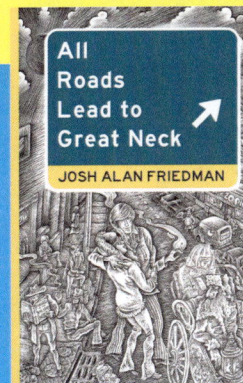

Attaché Case: Backstage at the Embassy, *memoir by* Todd Pierce

The Kitchen Confidential *of the State Department.* Opening up a famously tight-lipped profession, 28-year Foreign Service veteran Todd Pierce shares what it's like to serve as a working-level diplomat. As he explains in his preface, "This is a book by the help." Funny, revealing, pointed, and deeply human.

"Part memoir, part behind-the-scenes guide, and part ethnographic portrayal of the puzzling, opaque but never boring universe of American diplomacy, Attaché Case *is an irresistible page-turner, jam-packed with wit and insight. A pleasure to read."*

Stathis Kalyvas, Gladstone Professor of Government
and fellow of All Souls College, Oxford University

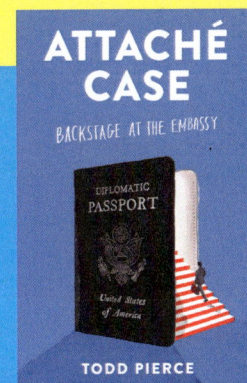

By Jorj: Georgette & Benjamin Harris Songsheet Art 1929–1948
Wyatt Doyle, Hal Glatzer, Peter Mintun,
Norman von Holtzendorff, *editors*

A breathtaking collection of vintage songsheet art by Georgette and Benjamin Harris, partners in art and life, and, as "Jorj," creators of some of the most beautiful, visually innovative, and memorable songsheets of the Jazz Age—and beyond.

new texture

www.ingramcontent.com/pod-product-compliance
Lightning Source LLC
Chambersburg PA
CBRC090216310326
41914CB00096B/1654